Ghosts and Phantoms
of Central England

by

Philip Solomon

PKN Publications, Willenhall, West Midlands, WV13 3QR, England

PKN Publications
Willenhall
West Midlands
England

Copyright © Philip Solomon 1997

First published in Great Britain
by PKN Publications, 1997

ISBN 1 872816 04 5

All rights reserved. No part of this publication
may be lent, resold, hired, reproduced or stored
in a retrievable system or transmitted in any form
whatsoever, nor by any other means electronic,
mechanical, photocopying, recording or otherwise
without the prior written permission of the author
and the publishers.

Printed in Great Britain by Goldthorn Press,
Bilston, England.

By the same author: -

Ghosts of the Midlands and How To Detect Them
Ghosts, Legends and Psychic Snippets
Black Country Ways in Bygone Days
Dreamers Psychic Dictionary

All available from PKN Publications

For my father Howard

and

Dedicated to all those who have helped me
at different stages of my life,
both alive and in Spirit

ACKNOWLEDGMENTS

Thanks to my wife Kath, for all help in typing of the manuscript and help with research.

Paul Saunders for photography and artwork.

Parnell for drawings and being a very good friend.

Express & Star Newspaper, especially Frances Cartwright.

Birmingham Evening Mail/Sunday Mercury.

Goldthorn Press Ltd., Bilston West Midlands, England, especially Ken Clarke.

Librarians throughout Great Britain for research and assistance and so much more, thank you all.

Marsha Barnes for always being my Number One supporter.

Finally, thanks to all the thousands of people who wrote of their experiences and are included in this book, also to those whose stories were not quite right for this edition. (In some instances pseudonyms have been used at the request of individuals to protect their identity).

PKN Publications
PO Box 141
Willenhall
West Midlands
WV13 3QR

CONTENTS

Foreword

Introduction

Chapter One - A Tour of the Haunted Midlands

Chapter Two - The A to Z of Ghosts

Chapter Three - A Toolkit for Ghost Hunters

Chapter Four - Ghosts From Further Afield

Chapter Five - The Most Haunted House in England's History

Chapter Six - Some Royal and Regal Ghosts

Chapter Seven - In Conclusion

Foreword

About the author and the book

I have known the author since he was a baby. Philip Solomon was born in Wolverhampton (New Cross Hospital, Wednesfield, to be precise) in July 1951. His mother, Elsie, had been a professional dancer and teacher of ballroom dancing. She was also a very fine medium who later became president of Darlaston Spiritualist Church. She passed away in 1987. His father, Howard, was in the haulage industry and, also at that time, developing a career as a promoter and running Rock'n'Roll dances throughout the Midlands. His father also developed into a medium and demonstrated at churches throughout Great Britain. He still gives readings to those that know him well at his bungalow in Willenhall, England.

I think it is a pretty obvious statement to say that Philip was always psychic and a natural born medium like those from a long line in his ancestry, but he has spent all his life researching all areas of the paranormal and New Age structure and is especially interested in astrology, methods of prediction, hypnosis and just about anything to do with the psychic world, quite rightly using the title Psychic Consultant. He was one of the very first people in the field to be employed to lecture in associated subjects by local education authority associations and still teaches such classes in Birmingham. He worked for three years solid as the resident freelance astrologer/psychic for BBC Radio at the Pebble Mill Studios, Birmingham, England and has written many major features for the Sunday Mercury, the Evening Mail and numerous other magazines and publications all over the world. He has perhaps become most famous for his annual New Year predictions published in Great Britain and America, which over the years have included the fall of the Berlin Wall, the peace agreement between Israel and PLO, the divorce of Prince Charles and Princess Diana, the separation of Prince Andrew and Duchess of York and even the life element possibilities that were found on Mars, always a year in advance - amazing!

Today he appears regularly on radio and television, gives talks and lectures and continues to write extensively for newspapers and magazines at home and abroad. He advises businesses, groups and gives private advice and readings to individuals and no doubt many of you who have bought this book will have met him in this way.

He continues to live in Wolverhampton, England, in the central Midlands, an area he loves. He is married and has two children, a boy and a girl. Of all the attributes and achievements, I for one, never lose interest in hearing his latest ghost stories, whether it is a haunting old or a haunting new, he always has a story to tell. In my opinion, if you are interested in ghosts, you cannot fail to be captivated and intrigued by this Midlands gazetteer of ghosts and hauntings.

Veronica Hart - Beverley Hills, California, USA.
But my ancestors actually came from Dudley!

Introduction

Why another Ghost Book? It seems I have written so many stories about hauntings and ghosts over the years for regional and national newspapers and talked about them on BBC Radio, television shows and other places, you would surely believe I had run out of stories to tell you! But I haven't you know. Almost every week someone tells me another one or perhaps asks my advice about a new haunting or ghost. In the pages of this book, I will of course tell you again of some of the very famous stories of the Midlands' haunted history, but there are also some that have never, ever been told before, only now when I have been given permission by those who have shared their experiences and in some cases, terror, with me.

I do believe in one way this book is quite unique in that it has been entirely put together, edited and researched by myself alone. Without wishing to sound big-headed, being recognised as a top psychic consultant and medium, both sides of the Atlantic, it would be very difficult for any individual to try to trick me into believing they had ghosts, or on a higher level, spirits present for publicity or other reasons, but I must tell you dear reader, plenty have tried and I have read so many well-known respected reports of ghosts that they have had me splitting my sides laughing at how gullible some of the less professional researchers really are. There again, as I have said, as a genuine medium, I do have a distinct advantage over most.

I decided a few years ago I would not really tie myself down to being part of a special organisation or society, although for a short period I did accept the role of president of the Ghost Hunters' Club of Great Britain and the Institute of Psychic Awareness, but equally quickly decided that for me research would be much more successful and appropriate with just a very small team of close friends and associates around me. In the pages of this book I will explain in very straightforward terms how to look out for ghosts, I suggest a very basic toolkit, and indeed, one or two very specialised pieces of equipment to assist your investigations and I will give you lots of other handy tips to assist you throughout but unless you are very experienced in the field it is best for you to join a club, society or group with people who know what they are doing and are both sensible and professional in their attitude to the paranormal. One word of warning, if you are young or inexperienced, and at any time at all something scares you, immediately leave well alone and pass the investigation or information of the circumstances on to a professional medium or advisor at your local spiritualist church who is sure to have people who can advise you.

Let me start off by telling you one thing in my view, ghosts are generally what survives of emotional memories of ordinary human beings, who, for whatever reason, pass over unexpectedly or tragically and are usually not aware they have passed over or died, if you like, and part of their personality carries on in the surroundings where they lived and died, sometimes keyed into an exact spot, time and place, but not always. A great mistake made by those who do not understand the subject is to mix up ghosts and spirits and think of them as the same thing. They are most certainly not. In the understanding of a real medium or professionally trained parapsychologist a ghost could be explained as being like a programmed robot incapable of reasoning, logic and divorced of any planning abilities at all, whereas spirits are on the step upwards that all of us make when passing through the veil of death's door, then carries on a full programme of existence on a higher dimension, thinking, reasoning and logically progressing appropriately, whilst the ghost can only repeat its last moments on earth over and over again and are nearly always completely harmless.

A lot of parapsychologists today are inclined to the belief that ghosts, spectres and other such manifestations take energy from the living to pass through our three-dimensional world. A big mistake made by so many people is to believe you only see ghosts at night. In my opinion, they have no reality of night or day, light or dark, they are always about, so to speak. It is a fact that mediums see them all the time when they place themselves in responsive mode. I have lectured and talked about all areas of the paranormal for many years, locally and all over the world, a favourite opening question to any talk wherever I am is: "Would you all put your hand up if you have seen a ghost?" In a class of let's say one hundred, the first show of hands will be about ten. I then ask the question again and say, "Come on, be honest!" It is up to about thirty-five by then. I then point out what I have just told you about ghosts being there all the time, even in the day. "OK then, who will accept they may have seen a ghost and not realised it?" I ask. It is then about ninety hands in the air. These statistics are true and it makes you think really, doesn't it?

Sometimes you will hear people talk about exorcising ghosts, I prefer the word rescue really, but very basically what others and I mean is that someone such as specialised clergy or a trance medium very simply explain to a ghost the reality of its position and predicament and advise it is time to be free from imprisonment. This could have been three months or three hundred years. If the ghost sees this to be its true position, wisely, but not always, it will be at the end of its haunting days, though the replay mode syndrome may be imprinted in the ether forever. Now I have made that sound very easy. It's not actually, but what I have told you is basically the crux of the matter, and it is never a job for amateurs or when you are on your own and in difficult cases must be conducted by a highly experienced professional trance medium in what those of us in the professional field call a rescue circle.

I will now tell you a little about different types of hauntings or ghostly characteristics. Some are certainly easier to categorize than others. Let me explain the top five symptoms of a haunting or ghost.

1. Apparitions - these are what you always hear about time and time ago and are reported in fifty percent of the cases that I have looked at. Some apparitions are so lifelike they are quite simply taken or believed to be living people, more typical though, are the transparent apparitions.

2. Footsteps - lots of hauntings will include footsteps in their reports. I have come across too many cases in my experience for them all to be explained as creaky, drying out floorboards, misunderstanding of the structure of buildings or misinterpretation of sounds. Footsteps which are often heard and reported by people we trust; policemen, firemen and others in authority who are trained to listen carefully and be perceptive, yet always objective in their view, cannot always be dismissed with a logical and earthly explanation.

3. The movement of objects and the similar - objects that unexplainably move around, large or small, are told to you by people who are undergoing unexplainable occurrences and perhaps in thirty percent of the cases professional investigators look into can usually find an answer to the doors that close on their own, but flying teapots and the switching on and off of computers, televisions, radios and other electronic equipment, has to and should be investigated.

4. Cold Spots - time and time again when you are investigating or looking into a ghost story you come across cold spots. In the past you could spot them straight away with simple thermometers. In parts of this book I will tell you about the equipment we have today that positively records them. Basically, more often than not cold spots equal something worth researching or investigating.

5. Dates or special times of the year - there are lots of ghosts in this book that seem to occur at regular intervals or special times of the year, some allegedly every 365th day without fail, it could be a type of tape recorded message possibility, locking into the ether and sensitives just play it back, in a sense, at the appropriate time!

In this book I have selected for you over one hundred and fifty cases from my files on the haunted areas of the English Midlands, some are historical in nature, others very modern and new, some quite unexplainable, but all equally intriguing and interesting stories of people of the area of which I love. Of course, each and every one of the stories to the best of my knowledge is the truth.

Chapter One

A Tour of The Haunted Midlands

Albrighton (Shrops)

Members of the Lycett family told me a story of the haunting of the Albrighton railway station. During the period of the Second World War a young airman arrived very late at the station and saw a middle-aged lady dressed in fine clothes pacing up and down the platform obviously, in his words, very upset and quite distraught. "Are you all right, madam?" asked the airman. "Yes, yes!" she snapped, "I'm waiting for my husband." Then turned and walked away and incredibly within six or seven feet from him vanished into thin air. According to the Lycett family, the young man was both upset and quite nervous about using that little railway station again, though he never saw anything else. Others have certainly seen, yet never communicated with, a similar lady, whom unfortunately it seems, waits for a train that is forever late!

Albrighton Railway Station, like most railway buildings, has ghost stories to tell

Albrighton. The Horns of Boningale has been dated back to the 17th Century, the stopping-off point for drovers going back and forth to market. Two well known spectres are the ghost of a lady who fell down the cellar steps and a ghostly old drover who considers the Horns to be his local. I also interviewed one of the young ladies who worked at the inn who told me that many strange things happened at the Horns and it was not at all unusual to see things, sense things, or even be tapped on the shoulder, yet for all that the atmosphere remains friendly.

White Ladies Priory. Local man, Bert Meek, told me of a strange experience he had in 1997. Apparently it is well known that if you laugh out loud in the centre of the ruins the sound will clearly echo back to you, but one late summer's evening, to Bert's amazement whilst trying this experiment, it was not the sound of his own laugh but the ghostly giggles of what sounded like several young girls that came back to him. He searched the area extensively but no one was to be seen. Why had his own laugh not returned? Very interesting! Others speak of the procession of ghostly white ladies on the narrow pathway that leads from the main road to the priory.

Boscobel House. Jack Smith was cycling past Boscobel House very early one morning when he saw what he describes as a group of Roundhead soldiers standing quite close to a pool that is near to the main road at the front of the house. Unusually, Jack feels that the soldiers actually saw him too, looking directly at him. A vision of the future for them perhaps? Who can say!

Alton (Staffs)

Alton Towers, you would never think when you take the kids on a day out to Alton Towers you are going to somewhere really haunted, would you? See if anything is still known of a story about fifty or sixty years ago concerning the steps of The Big House and the fairly regular appearance at that time of a gent dressed in top-hat, black cape and walking stick, usually accompanied by a large black dog. Also, the ghost of a lady apparently still recognised and well known to some of the present staff.

Ash Magna (Shrops)

Ash Magna, a spectral monk has been seen by several people on numerous occasions, standing at the entrance to Ash Grange apparently praying.

Bedworth (E. Mids)

Bedworth has a very strange apparition of a very old-fashioned funeral hearse pulled by black horses and driven by a wiry figure also dressed in black. This does seem to be a haunting that has been seen by a lot of people over a good many years, well before the Second World War right up to quite recently, indeed, about six months before this book was written by one of my correspondents, James Thompson. The strange thing about everyone who has seen this apparition is they also say it is only when the street is absolutely empty. It seems you have to be on your own to see it and also that there is an absolutely freezing cold atmosphere as the hearse passes by.

Have you seen a likeness of a black hearse and horses like this one?

Bentley (W. Mids)

Bentley near Walsall. Tracey, Steve, John and Sharon were all in their late teens when they saw Bentley's Laughing Cavalier on a hill by Bentley Church. In Steve's words, "It was absolutely like a real person except for the awful ghostly laugh. It chilled us all to the bone!"

The site of Bentley's Laughing Cavalier

Bewdley (Worcs)

Bewdley, has a strange haunting told to me by one of my correspondents, Mrs Doris English, where apparently her husband had a habit of missing the last bus from Kidderminster to Bewdley where he lived at that time. This would often be just after midnight. On one occasion he saw a little old lady dressed all in black walk past him on the road from Kidderminster to Bewdley. He said goodnight but no answer was returned and she simply disappeared. Apparently he ran all the way home to Bewdley. His parents advised him to forget it and just make sure he didn't miss the last bus again, but of course he did, and in the same place another strange occurrence took place. This time it was a galloping horse that cut across him and went over the hedge into the field and just vanished. But in truth these are not the only stories that I have heard of on that strange road between Kidderminster and Bewdley and this is not the first time I had heard the story of the little lady and the galloping horse either. Very interesting, but do they connect, that is the question?

Bilston (W. Mids)

Bilston, there have been some very reliable reports of the ghost of a woman dressed in a long black frock and bonnet and carrying a glowing lantern. She is said to appear fairly frequently in the area of Turles Hill. This would appear to be a long-standing haunting.

Bilston, a most unusual haunting allegedly occurs at the area of the old Meeting Road at Coseley, and was said to be haunted by the ghost of an old miner who frequently made his way at early morn and evening fall to some long-since lost and forgotten mine. One lady who wrote to me some years ago actually claimed she had spoken to the ghost.

Bilston, The Lunt council estate. Perhaps one of the most extraordinary ghost stories I have ever come across is that of a young couple, I will call them Tony and Tina for want of a better name, who were offered a council house in the vicinity of the Lunt Estate. Given the keys, they went to view the property and liked it very much indeed, until they went into the garden. In one corner stood a shed, painted in black and white stripes. Suddenly the doors flew open and out of the shed flocked what can only be described as hundreds of tumbler pigeons of all shapes and colours. Tina knew the type of birds they were because her brothers had kept similar birds at one time. They flew all round the garden and the couple and their two small children. Then in what seemed a few seconds the majority of them were flying in the sky and had left the place. The couple went back inside. "I'm not having those in the garden!" Tina said, walking into the kitchen and looking out of the back window. Suddenly she exclaimed, "Tony, Tony, they've all gone and you are not going to believe what I'm going to tell you, but so has the black and white shed!" The couple decided there and then to leave the property, this was one house they didn't want! I have known Tony for quite a few years and in truth he wouldn't even have had a problem with one or two ghosts, but hundreds of them flocking round you - well, that's the stuff of Alfred Hitchcock really, isn't it?

Birmingham

Aston Hall is said by some to be the Midlands most haunted house, perhaps even one of England's most ghostly buildings. An imposing Jacobean building with beautiful plasterwork, a great staircase and marvellous tapestries, it has so many ghosts that are accepted that the staff quite happily tell you about them. Some tell the tale of the ghost of John Holte who built the hall. Harsh, rough voices are often heard, loud bangs and heavy footsteps that some believe are the ghosts of soldiers long since past. Others tell of the ghost of May, the young daughter of Sir Thomas Holte, (you can see his picture hanging in the hall). May apparently fell in love with a lad from the lower classes. Her father forbade the relationship, let alone marriage and it is claimed May spent the rest of her life as a poor, demented creature. She is most often seen on the top floor in the area of the nursery. Some see her as a greyish mist, though many visitors to Aston Hall say they have seen May as a young, pretty, perfectly solidly formed figure. You may also be told the tale of a lady ghost of about fifty years of age. Some staff actually believe it is Mrs Walker, a servant at Aston Hall many years ago, and she is said to particularly enjoy a special chair that is on show at the hall even today. Indeed, one of my own relations, a famed lady medium, actually spoke to her and despite her capabilities, took the ghost for a living person until she vanished from the scene and the guide explained to the medium, "Oh, don't worry about it, she is our most resident ghost!" But of course these are just a few of the ghosts of Aston Hall.

Great Barr, regular reports of ghostly happenings at the corner of Chapel Lane and Crook Lane - reports which include spectral horses and some very strange and, at times, quite alarming noises.

Birmingham, Dudley Road Hospital has the ghost of a nurse known as Mary who makes herself known to patients, but only on very rare occasions to members of her own profession. There is also reports of the White Lady and a dark complexioned gentleman whom some nursing staff have said seemed so real they mistook him for a doctor on his rounds.

Janet Coleman of Birmingham told me a very interesting story of when, as a child, her mother and sister saw the vision of a lady's head, both on the television screen and on top of it. Janet, herself, saw the vision of the head a year later in the bedroom of the house in Wainwright Street, Aston, which was demolished some twenty-five years ago. She described the lady as blonde and smiling. Many years later her brother also admitted that he had seen the ghostly head. Apparently, at one time a young lady who had lived at this address hung herself following personal difficulties. As Janet says, could this be the reason that only the head without a body was seen?

Birmingham. I know many people in show business and even more from the modern music industry and because the people that generally are drawn into these professions are artistic sensitives, of course many, many ghost stories and tales of the supernatural are told to me. But one story in particular is both fascinating and extremely weird, to say the least. My friend, whom I will call Peter, had a very old Gibson guitar, very much like the one Chuck Berry uses on stage and, although Peter was very fond of this guitar, it was not one that he frequently used and would more often than not be on a stand in the corner of the room in which he practiced, composed music and made up lyrics, generally using a more modern guitar or a small electronic keyboard. One evening alone whilst searching for a riff (that's a collection of notes or a melody according to Pete) the old Gibson suddenly seemed to play one of these riffs for him on its own. Peter was certainly startled but being a musician, a very sensitive person and inquisitive, he listened very carefully as the guitar played the same set of notes over and over again. I have examined this guitar and could see nothing very special about it or feel anything with it really, and even as Pete says, it could have been his imagination but the melody line it influenced did, I can assure you, become part of a very successful song that would be known and recognised worldwide.

Birmingham. One of my correspondents, Diana, wrote to me about a musical jewellery box that frequently opened at night and played itself. At one time it had belonged to this lady's grandmother who gave it to her with items of jewellery and other little treasured mementos just before she passed away. One little brooch particularly attracted the attention of Diana's daughter Sarah, who always wanted it, but only being five her mother would not let her have it but promised one day it would be hers anyway. Diana occasionally went to a Spiritualist church and was told by a medium, "You have a jewellery box with a small brooch," describing exactly the one Sarah loved. "Would you give that brooch to a child?" asked the medium. Diana said she would and as soon as she got home immediately went upstairs to her bedroom and in truth and not to any real amazement was not surprised to see the lid open and the jewellery box playing. She took the brooch and closed the lid, came back downstairs and gave it to her daughter who has treasured it for the last twenty years. The only real disappointment to this story Diane says is that the box now never, ever plays and she only wishes it would on occasions!

Birmingham. Jenny Moore had a strange experience with an answer phone which, it would seem, was most attractive to a communicative ghost named Mary who had lived in Jenny's flat before her. Several of Jenny's friends complained that an old lady always answered the phone when she was out telling them, "This is my phone, I'm Mary. Who is this Jenny?" Even when the answering machine was set at two rings Mary would be there first before Jenny's playback message even had chance to start. A psychic friend apparently had advised Jenny on one or two points which included replacing the old phone with a new combined phone/fax/answering machine which would actually be quite useful in her part-time secretarial business and so far nothing spooky has happened since.

Harbourne, Birmingham. Dorothy Small had what can only be described as an ultra-modern ghostly experience, for it happened in connection with her PC Computer in the office where she worked as a secretary. The building she worked in had what you would call strange, unexplainable noises, bangs and footsteps that were heard by several members of staff. Stranger still, was the occasional rattle of an old manual typewriter that came from a completely empty office three doors down from where Dorothy and a younger colleague worked and both girls were quite convinced it was haunted. One day had been particularly difficult and Dorothy admits she was in a heightened state of bad temper and the old rattling Remington, as she called it, was really getting on her nerves. She barged down to the office and at the top of her voice shouted, "I am thoroughly sick of you and your typewriter! Why don't you go away?" and barged back out slamming the door behind her. Returning to her own office she sat down at her desk and looking at her monitor noticed a message had been typed on the screen which said, "Yes, and we're all thoroughly fed up with you too! Why don't *you* go away??" Other members of staff swore on their honour that they had not placed the message on her computer and Dorothy arranged for a medium friend of hers to visit the office and, although preferring not to give details of what happened, she said that proved to be the end of the matter.

The Crematorium at Yardley Cemetery in Birmingham was where a ghost was seen by Miss Cheryl Knowles, who in 1990 worked there as a cleaner. It was in the church area of the building that she saw an elderly man with his hands reaching out. either to keep his balance or ready to kneel to pray. As was her usual manner it was her intention to acknowledge and speak to the man, but as she looked again he had disappeared.

Many people from Birmingham say the wonderful town hall, built in 1834, is the ghostly walk of a Victorian gentleman dressed appropriately for the time. Also at times, a certain atmosphere that cannot be explained but was described to me by two persons of the highest integrity seemed like a time-slip experience to them.

Birmingham, The Repertory Theatre's hire department in Oozle Street has the ghost of a lady who apparently is rather fond of costumes, modern and medieval. They also, at one time, suffered strange odours that abounded in and around the building.

Birmingham, Barr Beacon which in the distant past is said to have been a hill used for Druid sacrifices. In recent years, good witnesses have claimed to have seen a very strange procession of Druid-like people slowly passing by in single file, also the sound of strange humming.

The Alexandra Theatre is allegedly the place you may see the vision of the former owner, Leon Salberg, who it is said puts in an appearance at dress rehearsals for new pantomimes. Some staff tell stories of taps on the shoulder from unseen hands and unexplainable cold spots. Indeed, at one time the Alex was claimed to be so haunted that a team of international ghost busters assembled to investigate the building.

Birmingham, New Street railway station is where you may see the vision of the Victorian gentleman in a top hat nicknamed Claude, who regularly puts in an appearance, especially round the month of October, and there have even been reports of him travelling on the trains and of being witnessed at Wolverhampton, Shrewsbury and Crewe at one time or another. Now a ghost that travels, that really is unusual!

Aston, Birmingham. In the year 1945 on a bomb site near the Lloyd's Bank on the corner of Lozells Road and Birchfield Road was where June Latham had a very strange experience. As a little girl she had been playing with other children and was at the top of one of the slopes on her own when she described suddenly seeing a mist all around her and very old gravestones. Being a child of only six she was very scared, when up walked a policeman and June jumped down into his arms, a very relieved little girl! For years after she told this story into adulthood but was never believed. However, in the 1960's with the demolition of the Aston suburbs underway, the Sunday Mercury did an article on Aston reporting that the area June had spoken of had been found to be the site of a lot of dug up bones. Examination of Birmingham's history proved that in the 1600's the site had indeed been a burial ground and churchyard. Did June Latham, as a little girl, have a time-slip experience? It is certainly a theory and a very interesting story.

Bloxwich (W. Mids)

Mr Morris wrote to me of a very strange experience he had as a young man, together with his mother, who both had the same experience of seeing an old black hearse drawn by jet black horses which trotted through the high street in Bloxwich and simply vanished as it passed them, remarkably seen again in 1997 by one of my correspondents who wrote to me describing exactly the same vision as Mr and Mrs Morris.

At the bottom of Bloxwich town there is a telephone box which is reported to have some very strange experiences. Apparently it has been known to ring as you walk past and actually speak your name. Very spooky that! But actually reported by several good witnesses.

Bridgnorth (Shrops)

Bridgnorth, The Theatre on the Steps was once an old chapel which is said to be haunted by a lady dressed in grey who has been seen by several people on the balcony of this lovely little theatre, yet when empty a place that can only be described as eerie to say the least!

Bridgnorth, the ghost of a young woman dressed completely in black is alleged to have appeared to a local policeman, standing in The Cartway and outside a greengrocers shop in the high street some years ago. The strange thing about this story is that I am told it was the vision of someone who was actually still alive and was so well known locally it made national TV and newspaper news at the time.

Bridgnorth, The Acton Arms at Morville has a haunted upstairs room. There is also the ghost of a priest who is said to travel the route of a former underground tunnel believed to be between the church and Morville Hall.

Bridgnorth, village of Astley Abbots. The ghost of Hannah Phillips is said to frequently appear in her bridal gown (she drowned in the River Severn the day before her wedding) in a layby situated between Severn Hall and The Boldings Farm. There are also reports of her husband to be, visions of a farmhouse that vanishes and the ghost of a lion. A very interesting village this.

The wedding basket of Hannh Pillips, which to this day is still displayed in Astley Abbots Church, Shropshire

Bridgnorth, the site where the old carpet factory stood on the banks of the River Severn is alleged to be haunted by the ghost of a monk known as "Old Mo". I have also had reports from a very good authority that the monk has also been seen in the area that leads up to the cable car that transports you from Low Town to High Town.

Bridgnorth, on the Highley Road from Bridgnorth, near Eardington village, is the site of a very strange haunting. Some years ago a young friend of mine reported being stopped in his car by a highwayman, who appeared to be quite human and solid, except that quite unexplainably, when challenged, vanished into thin air.

An illustration considerd to be an excellent likeness, by those that have seen the Highley Highwayman

Brierley Hill (W. Mids)

Brierley Hill, actually almost in Stourbridge, this Black Country town has a public house known as the Starving Rascal that is so haunted by a tramp who died on the steps after being refused food that they renamed the old place after him. They also get wet footprints that just won't away and other ghosts a-plenty! The former landlord, Phil Nichols, always claimed it was the most haunted pub in the Midlands and the present owners also say regulars have what can only be described as interesting and spooky tales of ghostly goings-on to tell!

Broseley (Shrops)

Broseley, Edinburgh House, Broseley Wood, is said to be the site of a haunting by a female form which appears dressed in grey with a large silver key hanging from her waist.

Brownhills (Staffs)

Brownhills, a new and strange story of the ghost of a young woman who has been seen in the area in and around the open market apparently quite unaware of being viewed as she slowly floats by.

Cannock (Staffs)

Cannock, Hawks Green Lane. Several reports of people hearing the sound of horses hooves and of riders shouting to one another, sometimes in the road and at other times in a nearby field.

Cannock. I will tell you a story and a ghostly experience an old mining relative of mine had several years ago. In the family we call it the Two-Bob Double ghost story. Apparently, the old chap had been out walking in the area known as Chasetown with a couple of his terrier dogs late one night when he saw an even older man with what looked like a whippet dog walking quite some way in front of him. Focused upon the figure he noticed that he dropped a small object from his hand as he walked along. On reaching it my relative noticed it was quite a pretty little pink box and called to the man, "Oi! You've dropped something." But he either didn't hear him or just ignored him and carried on walking further into the distance, despite my relative calling him time and again. He picked up the box and looked inside. All that was there was a little piece of paper with the name of two race horses written on it in the form of a bet, yes, a two-bob double, as they called it at that time. Being superstitious, that night he looked in the paper to see if they had won, but neither of them had even a mention of their names. He looked at the racing lists for the following day and again, neither of them were listed to run. By Saturday he had almost forgotten about his find but turning to the racing page of his morning paper he saw them there. Richard of Bordeaux in the Mackeson Gold Cup and a horse called Cash in the Mackeson Hurdle, so he backed them with two bob in a double, that's ten pence in today's money by the way, and they won at the amazing odds of 20-1 and 50-1 and that Saturday evening, my relative had quite a bit of cash-in-hand and was a happy man indeed. A coincidence or a bit of ghostly racing insight and good luck? Well, what can I say - you decide!

Cannock. An unusual ghostly going-on happened several times to a local bobby some years ago always by the cinema in Cannock. Just as he reached that part of town he would hear the sound of a Lambretta or Vespa-type scooter pull up right outside the building but would never have any sight of the machine or person. This happened regularly over a period of about three weeks, then nothing more at all. The young policeman and others also heard this machine in and around Cannock town itself. It is particularly interesting to me because I have actually heard this for myself outside the cinema.

Castle Ring near Cannock Chase is said to have several ghosts which include a pretty young girl who sits weeping and of the apparitions of monks. Cannock Chase has been the site of many ghosts. Over the years people have reported seeing cavaliers and roundheads, very large cats as big as pumas, indeed, perhaps they are pumas (real ones according to some people!) and figures dressed in various religious regalia a-plenty!

Halfway between Cannock and Rugeley there is a fishing pool, this is the site apparently of several strange apparitions, one is particularly interesting. reported in 1990 by Peter Berry, who says he saw a strange man in a broad-brimmed hat and old-fashioned clothing who carried a stave which he seemed to bang on the ground to gain Peter's attention then just vanished before his very eyes.

Cosford (Shrops)

Cosford, the R.A.F. Museum. Reports of an RF398 Bomber aeroplane being haunted by the ghost of a former Spitfire pilot or of an engineer who committed suicide quite nearby around 1940 seem to be too many in number to be completely disregarded. In very recent times I have also had reports of the sound of a pistol being fired that cannot be accounted for or explained.

Coventry

Coventry, the Belgrade Theatre I've been told, has had several strange "goings on" that could be worthy of any ghost hunter. Why not start by asking the staff who work there about the actors and actresses who never get paid? Perhaps it's the enchantment of show business and grease paint that they just cannot bring themselves to leave behind.

The Old Dyers' Arms in Spon End is apparently one of Coventry's oldest pubs and in the opinion of some correspondents, one of its most haunted with the cellar its most mysterious and heightened position for activity. Barrels and other objects are alleged to roll around of their own accord and to have spooked staff in the past, though other people have had strange experiences in other rooms in the public house. Apparently the lads even have to be a little coy in the gents, where a young girl is known to have a peek and then quickly disappear as the men rearrange themselves, after what comes naturally as they say! Mrs Barbara Goddard, the present landlady, also told me she has had the gas turned off unexplainably on one or two occasions.

Coventry, wherever you go in the world people know of the story of Lady Godiver and Peeping Tom. My historian friends tell me it has far more to do with legend than real history. Yet for all that several people have written to me claiming to have seen a beautiful lady riding naked on a white horse who allegedly last rode through the streets of Coventry in the early hours of the morning just after England won the World Cup in 1966. Was it a ghost or was it a real person? Well friends, you tell me!

Coventry Theatre is claimed to be haunted by many people who have worked there in the past but a white lady and a gentleman in top hat are said to be the ones most regularly reported. Eventually the theatre became a bingo hall and some correspondents say they have seen the man tapping his stick outside the old theatre and that it is a lucky omen.

Darlaston (W. Mids)

Joan Ward wrote to me about her experiences on the buses of the Midland Red service, telling me that many passengers that were picked up would then inexplicably vanish and that all the old drivers and clippies could tell you similar stories but don't for fear of ridicule. Once on the Darlaston to Willenhall run Joan said a man and what appeared to be his wife, hailed the bus in full view of the driver, stepped on at the rear, took a seat halfway down the aisle and then basically dematerialised before her very eyes! The drivers and clippies used to call this particular couple Bill and Bertha and Joan assures me that her bus was not the only one that this couple took for a ride.

Darlaston, Owen Road, close to the entrance of the old Rubery Owen factory. I am told that the ghost of a young girl with long blonde hair, dressed in a white, flowing dress has been seen on numerous occasions to cross from one side of the road to the other, sometimes stopping to smile at an individual before vanishing in front of his or her eyes. Several people actually wrote to the local newspaper claiming to have seen this girl around about 8.30 in the morning. Could she have been on her way to work at one of the nearby factories in a vision of a former existence?

Derby

Derby, The Howard Hotel, Friargate, while under renovation, was reported to be under poltergeist-type attacks and screams. Interesting because looking at old maps, on the site of the hotel around 1770 there was a prison there where many a person met their grisly end. Perhaps there lies the answer!

Dudley (W. Mids)

Dudley, Evans Halshaw Rover Dealers. One of their reception staff, some years ago, told me a very interesting story about car registrations. "Do you believe some are unlucky?" she asked. "I suppose it depends on who has the vehicle," I replied. It seems they once had a vehicle that had the number 666 as part of its registration and apparently it was always trouble, to coin a phrase, and always acted oddly whatever was done to it. "Ask that mechanic over there," said one of the receptionist's colleagues. He said, "I'd rather not talk about it, mate. An absolute beast that one was." Or words and expletives to that effect! Yet recent research and converstion with the present staff suggests it was more likely the number 666 was actually on the chassis of a car. Whichever way you look at it, mind, a strange story.

Dudley, the ancient and historical castle and its surrounding grounds has had many reports of hauntings of all kinds. Reports of historical characters and perhaps more interestingly, recently the ghosts of a gentleman and lady dressed in the style of the early Thirties, appearing in and around the castle grounds and zoo. My friend, director of tourism, Keith Cheetham, organises ghost walks in this area but a strange occurrence is whenever I take any of my students on this walk they all seem to see ghosts that are not actually on the itinerary. Other reports include the Grey Lady seen in and around the castle area, a monk dressed in a black habit and soldiers, an historian colleague, seeing his first ghosts, tells me they were definitely Royalists. Hmm! Interesting.

A section of the walkways at Dudley Zoo where a ghostly couple are said to stroll

Dudley, The Black Country Museum, near Tipton, is said to have a most unusual ghost, one that is sensed in the old pub called The Bottle and Glass they have rebuilt, which formerly stood in Brierley Hill Road, Brockmoor. In my experience it is not usual for ghosts to travel but perhaps the pub had a ghost at its former site that has been absorbed into the atmosphere of the walls or, indeed, the very bricks that it was built with. Members of the management had spoken to me of strange goings on and noises in the cellar. When I visited the building, Mr Derek Willcox, the landlord, told me that several people had certainly seen and sensed things at his lovely old pub. A most interesting haunting indeed. Mr Willcox also told me of the talk of a haunting in the area of the old chemist. So those of you interested in ghosts, when you visit this wonderful museum of Black Country history, should certainly keep a look out for spooky happenings!

The Bottle and Glass Inn rebuilt at the Black Country Museum

Edgehill (Warks)

Warwickshire, Edgehill is the site of the famous English battle of 1642, now frequently refought by ghostly armies in the sky, often around Christmas time and witnessed by people in groups as well as on their own.

Enville (Shrops)

Enville. The ghost of a small black boy, or man according to some witnesses, has been seen on occasions to run right through the centre of the village and at other times the surrounding fields of Enville, throwing his arms in the air as though he has won a race or something similar.

Derek Whitehouse had a strange experience of hearing, in the middle of the night, what he described as typical fairground sounds, the laughter of people and other sounds and music that you would associate with such an event, yet in his words, definitely from another era or time.

Fairgrounds and older places of entertainment seem to attract ghosts

Reports of the ghosts of a former lord and his lady of the manor appearing in and around the area of Enville and sometimes seen walking on the nearby Kinver Edge just seem too numerous to be rejected. Locals tell a tale of an earl and his gypsy girl. The grounds of the rectory at Enville is also said to be haunted by a ghost described as having the appearance of a latter day butler, yet others have claimed he wears the attire of a footman, also of a very pretty young girl described by one lady as what she would call an upstairs maid.

Hednesford (Staffs)

Cross Keys, Hednesford is allegedly on occasions visited by the ghost of someone locals feel was put to death by the legendary Staffordshire murderer, Dr Palmer.

Ironbridge (Shrops)

Ironbridge, Telford, The Tontine Hotel. One of the rooms in the hotel is said to be definitely haunted and people have been known to insist on being moved after a restless night with unexplained goings-on!

Jackfield (Shrops)

Jackfield, Telford. The old red church is, unfortunately, now nothing more than a ruin, that stands in a field which at one time served as the burial ground following the plague of cholera. Local people claim they have seen the ghost of a lady dressed in what appears to be a long cloak, bonnet and carrying a lighted lantern. I am told that many years ago locals reported seeing shadowy figures in the windows when there was definitely no one there!

Kenilworth

Kenilworth Castle has lots of ghosts who are said to include a lady who sits sewing, dressed in clothes belonging to the fourteenth century and of several cowled, religious figures walking and talking together.

Kenilworth, The Talisman Theatre, has a history of ghosts which include the Grey Lady and the slight figure of a hooded monk who seems to put in appearances in various parts of the building to those receptive of his vision and then simply vanishes before their eyes.

Kidderminster (Worcs)

Kidderminster, The Staffordshire Building Society has a most unusual ghost that the staff have nicknamed Polly, basically because she just keeps putting the kettle on! Middle-aged Polly is often seen in period costume, a long off-white embroidered dress. Mr Shiv Ahluwalia the shop manager, however, has no problems with the ghost, describing her as friendly, telling the local newspaper, "We've got no problems at all with Polly putting the kettle on!"

Kidderminster, Harvington Hall, this is a place where many people claim to have seen the ghost of a witch, or at least a lady they claim to have been a witch, hanged at the crossroads outside, that she now appears to forever haunt.

Kinlet (Worcs)

Kinlet, the Hall at Kinlet and its surrounding areas is said to be haunted by Sir George Blount who died in 1581. His ghost was seen at one time to come up from a pool in the grounds of Kinlet Hall on horseback, enter the great dining room and leap over the table as his family looked on, but has not been seen in recent years until last year when several young people reported seeing such a figure in the early hours of the morning in the grounds of the building.

Kinver (Staffs)

Kinver, in the Gibbet Lane area is the ghost of a horseless highwayman, guilty in his lifetime of the most awful crime of murder, a ghost that has been seen by many people over the years and actually seen by members of my own family.

There is an area just a little way from the village of Kinver known as "The Compa" which is said to be haunted by a ghost called Old Joe, a former land worker. At one time a local couple called Reg and Jean were so aware of Old Joe, that they actually set a place for him at the dinner table!

Shatterford near Kinver. Albert Jones tells me of a vision and the sound of a very powerful red Triumph motorcycle that came up behind his lorry in Compton, Kinver, followed him down the lane towards Shatterford and passed him taking a sharp bend a little further ahead, just out of the lorry driver's view.

Just at that moment Mr Jones heard a very large bang and was quite positive a serious accident had occurred. He stopped his vehicle, quickly jumped out and ran round the bend to see if he could help. To his amazement and relief nothing at all was there. Was this the enactment of an incident that had happened some years before? It is a possibility, but the locals tell me they are not aware of such an incident in that area ever happening.

Leicester

Leicester, Bosworth Hall is a long-standing site of hauntings and strange "goings-on" including an unremovable red stain which always feels moist, a priest and a fine lady.

Lichfield (Staffs)

Hanch Hall, Lichfield, is owned by the Wolves' assistant manager, Colin Lee and his wife Linda, and is reported to have several ghosts, one of them an elegant lady, another a pretty serving wench. There are also strange perfumes that abound.

Lichfield, The King's Head Hotel in St John's Street is alleged to be the site of a haunting known locally as The Laughing Cavalier.

Lichfield Cathedral over the years has been a place that several people have written to me claiming to have seen what they describe as ghosts, not surprisingly generally dressed in religious clothing, and are seen both inside and outside the building.

Little Hay near Lichfield is where a very strange occurrence happened to a highly respected policeman some years ago. Being a plasterer in civic life he had volunteered to help the owners of a little cottage in the village to renovate it. However, perhaps a former owner was not so keen for the policeman to help with the renovation, for whenever he poured water into a bucket ready to mix the plaster it simply vanished before his eyes. The owners decided the cottage was haunted and mediums were called in but without a successful result. Ultimately, the ghost was laid when a clergyman simply prayed at the cottage and apparently, apart from the occasional smell of fragrant lavender, nothing now remains to tell of the case of the vanishing water.

Long Compton (Warks)

Long Compton, The Rollright Stones, a Bronze Age circle in Warwickshire has its fair share of ghosts, a history associated to witches and perhaps at one time great religious significance. Check out the legend of the king accompanying knights that were all turned to stone; the sorcery of witches and warlocks. Locals tell me there are stories of hooded figures, perhaps ancient Druids, walking in procession up to and around the stones. A correspondent, Malcolm Peters, also tells me that one windswept night he and two friends certainly saw the figures of several beautiful but ghostly young naked girls all with long flowing hair dancing in the centre of the stones quite unaware of the young men who stood there watching for several minutes.

Warwickshire, Long Compton is supposedly haunted by a coach and horses in the area of Harrow Hill.

Ludlow (Shrops)

Ludlow, The Bull Inn has a certain atmosphere that is worth a visit for that experience alone. Several tenants over the years have claimed that strange occurrences do happen within that inn. Locals tell of the ghost of a woman who always makes herself known to "fresh 'uns" as they put it to me in their Shropshire brogue!

Ludlow, The Feathers Hotel at Ludlow is a seventeenth century building, a pretty well investigated haunted house and it is where a sales rep saw the ghost or doppelganger of a pretty young lady who was still alive! Spooky but very true.

Ludlow, The Globe is said to be haunted by many ghosts including a man wearing a cloak and wig. Also, a figure wearing a nightshirt, carrying a candle in a brass holder. There have also been reports of old-time soldiers seen in the vicinity of the inn.

Ludlow Castle is very eerie, the one time home to the little princes before their journey to the Tower of London. Also the tormented ghost of Marion de la Bruyere who throws herself from the battlements of the so-called Hanging Tower. There is also nearby a large house open to the public where the owner said he had seen a figure exactly like the likenesses painted of Queen Ann

Boleyn. I certainly sensed ghosts, but were perhaps more likely to be the former distant residents of the house.

Milford (Staffs)

Milford, on the Rugeley Road, near a place called Weetman's Bridge, there is allegedly a phantom cyclist who appears and just as quickly vanishes before your very eyes.

Much Wenlock (Shrops)

Much Wenlock, Wenlock Edge has numerous ghosts which include monks, ghosts that step out in front of cars, time-slip experiences, engined vehicles cutting out for no apparent reason and strange experiences at various times of the year.

Netherton (W. Mids)

The Boat Inn, St Peter's Road, Netherton, was closed in 1987, but according to one of my correspondents, Mr Clifford Green, certainly had a history of being haunted. At that time the manager was Les Horn, the ex-West Bromwich Albion player. Mr Green said that he had known glasses break without explanation and that people had felt taps on their shoulder, he himself had been prodded in his left shoulder blade that could not be explained. Other correspondents have written to me in the past about the Boat and that if it did have a ghost they felt it was a man who had probably actually some connection to the site the Boat was built on. One lady also told me of a strange combination of smells, something between fish and aromatic tobacco.

Netherton, the area that is known as Bumble Hole is alleged to be the former home of the so-called Dudley Devil - Theophillus Dunn. There is also a strange windmill where one person told me they had seen the vision of a Viking warrior and that the windmill was on a special or magical site although I found no real evidence to support this possibility.

Nottingham (E. Mids)

Nottingham, Colgrave Colliery. A phantom wearing protective clothing and hat has been seen by several of the miners and is often seen as a warning in some way to be extra careful that day or night.

Nottingham Castle is haunted by the ghost of Queen Isabella who is seen roaming aimlessly, searching for her lover.

Nottingham, Linby, Newstead Abbey has a ghost known as Goblin Friar, bringer of bad tidings. The house is also associated with the Byrons who allegedly suffered much bad luck here and the spectre of the lord's hound, Boatswain, has been seen at night's fall.

Nuneaton

Nuneaton, Watling Street separates Nuneaton and Hinkley and is where several good reports have been made of a highwayman wearing a three-cornered hat and coat. Some say this is the ghost of Dick Turpin or a very similar character.

Tony and Claire of Nuneaton had a strange experience in 1996 driving home after a visit to Tamworth Castle. Earlier that week they had purchased a new car with a radio which Tony was finding a bit complex to use - basically he couldn't get it to work. Unexplainably, on their return journey the radio lit up, switched on and a voice said it was best to avoid the motorway at all costs as very heavy congestion was likely. It then played some light music for a few minutes and switched off again. "That's lucky, especially as the radio isn't working properly," commented Tony and they used minor roads to return home. Upon their arrival home, Tony noticed a large lump was spreading on one of the tyres where an imminent blow-out looked most likely. He took the car in for a tyre change the next day and asked the mechanic to look at the radio. "There's no wonder it's not working, guv, the speakers aren't plugged in." "But I had a message on it and some music," answered Tony. Now this could have a simple answer but on the other hand was it a psychic message to save them from mishap or injury? It makes you think, doesn't it?

Camp Hill Working Men's Club Nuneaton where one of the members wrote to me telling me of a very interesting story of the club having the ghost of a former barmaid putting in an occasional appearance and also of an upstairs room that can only be described as having a full scale party going on, or at least it sounded that way, until this person opened the door and found the room to be absolutely empty and not a person in sight. There have been other reports of a young man dressed in Rock'n'Roll clothes and the sounds of an old British motorcycle outside the building, my correspondent describing it as sounding like an old BSA or Norton would have sounded in the 50's or 60's.

Old Hill (W. Mids)

Old Hill, the site of the former Cherry Orchard, close to Waterfall Lane, is the scene of the alleged ghost of a Scotsman reputedly killed for his gold. He walks the area dressed in seventeenth century clothes with a pouch holding his gold attached to his wrist.

Haden Hill House. Correspondent, George Leek, told me of his experiences some time ago of seeing two ghosts at this building, one a lady in a white mist on the stairs and of a man in black of Victorian appearance and dress, carrying a stick. Interestingly, other witnesses have told very similar stories that give a good deal of credence to Mr Leek's claim.

Rowley Regis (W. Mids)

Rowley Regis, the site of the old Hales Abbey is haunted by the ghost of a priest who is said to have broken his holy vows by falling in love with a local woman, and has been seen walking and praying. The woman is said to appear wringing her hands and crying.

Rugby (Warks)

Warwickshire, Kings Newnham Tower near Rugby certainly has a very long history and claims of being haunted. Many years ago the coffins and bodies of aristocratic people were discovered in a flooded vault nearby. Evidence suggested that some of the bodies had been embalmed and had remained in good condition but the majority were nothing more than skeletons. One skeleton appeared to have had its head removed from its body and had perhaps come to a violent end. It seems these people were reburied where they had been found with appropriate ceremony and should be resting peacefully and yet reports are given of a tall dark man that carries a large candle who seems to be searching for something no one can see, three beautiful ladies, a grey lady and of screams and roaring sounds that are offensive and scary to beast and man alike. Did something violent happen here at some time that sensitives and psychics pick up on?

Rugeley (Staffs)

The Shrewsbury Arms at Rugeley according to one of my correspondents is the haunt of no other than the famed practitioner of poison, Dr Palmer, who has been known to put in the occasional appearance, although as I understand it not in recent years. In fact, my research suggests the ghost is more likely to be of a John Parsons-Cook (a Palmer victim) whose post-mortem actually took place at the building. Other locals speak of another doctor-type character walking the nearby streets in the hours of darkness, again not thought to be Palmer, and quite grimly described as Doctor Dark.

This is how the illustrator sketched what could have been the phantom known to some as Doctor Dark of Rugeley

The site of Ravenhill House on the A51 midway between Rugeley and Brereton had at one time been a temporary hospital for British soldiers of the First World War. A person wrote to me who had associations with the house many years ago and claimed that it was not unusual for visitors to see the vision of a kindly, sympathetic nurse of those times, moving in and around the rooms apparently still carrying on with her duties. I am also told of the vision of an elderly lady kneeling or sitting staring into the fire of an old-fashioned fireplace, yet this is a fleeting vision, for the minute that you see her, she disappears before your very eyes. There are also reports of galloping horses, coaches and a rather strange report sent to me of a ghostly voice shouting out, "Halt! Who goes there?" But surely that would be more relevant to the Second World War than the time of ghostly horses and coaches. Ravenhill is certainly interesting.

Shifnal (Shrops)

Shifnal. Many years ago an auntie of mine told me of the time she and a friend visited the home in Shifnal of her late maiden aunt. The house had been uninhabited for some weeks and having no close family to sort things out everything had been left pretty much as it was on the day she had passed away. She had even left a prepared coal fire ready to be lit, pieces of paper wrapped into firelighters, little bits of wood placed on the top and chunks of coal placed on top of that. In truth, coal was what had brought my aunt and her friend to the house that evening as at this time there was a great shortage of fuel in Wolverhampton where they lived and this lady had a large supply of coal in the cellar to which they were quite sure she would welcome them to take whatever they could carry before the property fell into the hands of strangers, so down the cellar they went. Its darkness only brightened by a small flickering candle, they gathered the coal a lump at a time until eventually they both came back up with a full shopping bag each. They blew out the candle and turned into the living room where they had the shock of their lives, before them in the old black fireplace, burning quite brightly and filling the room with light, was the fire they had seen prepared on their earlier entrance to the house, quite clearly lit by unseen hands. The two ladies looked at each other, dropped the bags where they stood and fled, never to return. Yet to me it always seemed a silly action that they took. Surely it was only our ancestral aunt's welcoming way of warming them up a bit.

Shifnal, the Naughty Nell public house is a very haunted site - a place that I have personally investigated myself and have no doubt is a site of special interest. Reports suggest figures from another age are seen, a male publican and serving wenches, things move around, strange noises, and unexplained, unusual fragrances have been known to fill the air. The very first time I visited there, acting as a medium, I told the owner I had a feeling there was a connection to a Mr Rudge in the distant past and that there were tunnels under the building. Subsequent investigations proved my feelings were right. A Mr Rudge did have associations to the inn and there were tunnels that have recently been discovered. Several tradesmen found this building so strange and saw so many unexplainable things during its recent restoration that many of them flatly refused to work there and this brought both newspapers and professional psychic investigators' groups to the building. In my opinion, the building is haunted, but it is an absolutely friendly and pleasant place to be and not at all scary in any way, unless you are one of those people that are scared of all ghosts, that is.

Naughty Nell - a very haunted building

Shortheath (W. Mids)

Shortheath near Willenhall. Two friends I have known for many years from my school days told me a story of their uncle who lost his mind following an experience at the top of Clarks Lane, Shortheath where there is a small bridge that at one time had a canal running under it. Apparently their uncle had been a very clever young man with a good career before him until one evening he walked across this bridge and saw a black cat with green glowing eyes staring at him. If this man had one failing it was that he had an unnatural hate of cats. Grabbing the creature he flung it over the bridge and walked on laughing to himself, when suddenly behind him he heard the heavy rattling of chains and a strange hissing sound. The noises got louder and closer, to the stage where he did panic and run. However, the sounds seemed to go with him and got closer and louder still, especially the heavy rattling of chains, until it was right behind him, but still he ran until finally exhausted he fell to the ground. There before him stood an entity that for the rest of his life he flatly refused to speak about except to say it pointed at him. From that moment on and for the rest of his life he remained a mumbling fool, often laughed at by the local community, indeed, a poor shadow of his former self. As kids we often spoke to this man and he would finish anything he said by warning us against cruelty towards the animal kingdom. As a friend of his nephews I, perhaps more than the other boys, listened to his stories and took heed!

Shrewsbury (Shrops)

Shrewsbury, Abbey Foregate. People who lived in Abbey Foregate have reported hearing tapping and banging noises. Many claim this is relevant to the ghost of an old cobbler called Harry.

Shrewsbury, The Dun Cow is said to be the site of a grey hooded figure some people have seen walk through walls. Also the site, strangely enough, of a Dutch cavalry officer in full uniform.

Royal Shrewsbury Hospital. Some of the nurses told me there have been reports of the vision of a monk being seen in and around the hospital site and of the unexplained fragrance of lavender. The hospital itself was only built about twenty-five years ago, but could it have been built on the site of an older building with people associated with a religious order?

Shropshire

Willey, the churchyard is haunted by the ghost of Tom Moody, a local horseman of great repute and legend.

Stiperstones, Shropshire, is haunted by the ghost of Wild Edric who has been seen on horseback leading his followers. Strangely enough, this often precedes times when Great Britain would be going to war. The Stiperstones is also said to be haunted by witches and there is a legend that all the ghosts of Shropshire appear on a certain night of the year. Nearby is also the Devil's Chair, a large collection of rocks, where legend says the Devil sits and it is unadvisable to stay there too long, for if you do a terrible storm often occurs.

Madeley, in the churchyard, several people have reported seeing the ghost of a frail old lady, usually early in the morning at first light, yet not at all frightening.

Solihull (W. Mids)

Solihull, Baddesley Clinton, Knowle. Many good reports of strange and unexplained manifestations occurring in this medieval moated Manor House on a very regular basis include the apparitions of former owners, a priest and a fair-haired woman in black, to mention just a few.

Smethwick (W. Mids)

Smethwick, Warley. Brenda Smith had a strange experience in the early hours of New Year's Day, 1994. Switching the television set off at about 12.45 a.m., she noticed a small very bright spot of light in the centre of the screen. Like most of us have done at one time or another, she gave the set a sharp tap. At that very moment, according to this very down-to-earth and honest lady, a voice clearly said, "Good night Bren, happy New Year."

Stafford

Shugborough Hall is allegedly haunted by a former lady of the manor, the good lady Harriet, who apparently was quite regularly seen by one former member of staff. The building is also said to have several cold spots, the unexplained fragrance of old-fashioned perfumes, aromatic tobacco, cheese and fish.

Eccleshall Castle at Stafford according to Mrs Doreen Grayson has some very strange goings on. She tells me of the legend of a grey lady, a white lady, a spectral cavalier and of a strange looking black dog that apparently is most likely to alert you of danger at dusk and early morning. All of these things are seen round the grounds of the castle site.

The artist's impression of what the White Lady may look like

Stratford-upon-Avon (Warks)

The Royal Shakespeare Theatre, Stratford, has a ghost that some members of the staff know as the Lady in White and has been described as a typical ghostly apparition. Another couple wrote to me speaking of a strange experience of sitting next to a young couple dressed in what they described as the clothes of the Sixties era, who inexplicably disappeared. Very strange that! Strange noises, the movement of glasses and other unexplained occurrences are also said to happen in the Balcony Bar.

Stratford, Alcester Road. Nearby to The Shottery turning reports of a time-warp occurrence involving ghostly Roman soldiers that go noisily marching by!

Stratford, Hathaway Lane, The Shottery, is famous for its regular ghostly visitor that takes objects, then carefully puts them back again.

Ann Hathaway's cottage, Stratford-upon-Avon, a building that is certainly said to have funny goings-on, so to speak!

Clopton House, Stratford-upon-Avon has many ghosts according to a correspondent who spent much time at this site before it was refurbished in the 1970's. I am told that the women of the Clopton family have a history of misfortune and bad luck, some of them in the extreme. Legend has it that Charlotte Clopton, in 1564 had been buried alive. Others had committed the awful act of suicide rather than accept arranged marriages and give up the love of their lives. There are even reports that the great playwright himself, William Shakespeare puts in an appearance at this building. Could it have been his inspiration for Romeo and Juliet? Ah, to be or not to be a ghost, that is the question!

Stoke-upon-Trent (Staffs)

Handley, Stoke, just between Etruria and Handley the ghost of a large white rabbit has been observed to jump from one side of the road, run to the other side and completely disappear at a spot known as "The Grove".

Checkley Rectory has allegedly been haunted for many years by Mrs Hutchinson, wife of Rev William Hutchinson who died in 1878. Apparently something of a tyrant in life, some say she continued to make matters difficult for the villagers even after her death in 1895.

Stourbridge (W. Mids)

A Victorian couple, immaculately dressed in very dark clothing, supposedly stroll the main streets at Christmas, one correspondent claiming the ghostly gent even lifted his hat to him! Strangely, I have received the same report in nearby Halesowen and in my experience it is unusual for ghosts to travel at all. Very interesting.

Sutton Coldfield (W. Mids)

Sutton Coldfield, Bishop Vesey's Grammar School. Mr John Rogers was a pupil there in the late thirties and early forties and tells me that doors would often open and close of their own accord and certainly there was a reputation at that time that Bishop Vesey's ghost would walk the halls now and again. Mr Rogers also said that in the company of others he actually witnessed five doors open and shut in front of him and asked if it could have been Bishop Vesey's ghost that did so.

The Three Tuns Pub, Sutton Coldfield, was according to one of my correspondents, Mr Bill Drew, reportedly haunted by a ghostly cavalier. The story had so much credence that at one time apparently BRMB Radio actually sent a ghost busting team to investigate, but to Bill's question as to whether there have been any sightings of the cavalier lately - well, not to my knowledge.

Tamworth (Staffs)

Tamworth, Tamworth Castle is a very haunted place. Here you will find the ghost of King Alfred's daughter, Editha, and the White Lady, often alleged to have been seen by staff and visitors alike and it is a place that is regularly investigated by researchers of the paranormal, some of whom say on record undoubtedly this is indeed a most strange site.

Telford (Shrops)

Telford. The Blists Hill Museum. Mary and Mick McCarthy had a ghostly experience at an event that had been set up to create exactly that illusion, one winter's evening in 1996, an event called Blists Hill Ghostly Gaslight, but that night Mick and Mary feel sure they met a real ghost. They had just gone past the chemist shop in the recreated high street when they saw a man of about fifty or sixty in a farmer's frock and what looked like a very long white pipe in his mouth and carrying a long stick. The only thing that would make you realise everything was not as it should be was that he didn't seem to appear to Mick and Mary not to have any feet or ankles and duly walked straight through a nearby brick wall. They were astonished and thought it was an absolutely fabulous special effect they had just witnessed and asked one of the workers how such a feat or trick was possible. The guide told them quite frankly that he had no idea what they were talking about and certainly no one in such dress was on duty that night. Considering all the evidence I think the only conclusion you can come to is that at some time the Blists Hill Museum may actually have been a farm and Mick and Mary had been there at just the right time that a real ghost decided to put in an appearance at this themed ghostly event.

Tipton (W. Mids)

Tipton, the Noah's Ark public house in the centre of Tipton town was once the home of a legendary local boxing hero and his wife. During their time as tenants, it is stated that they were haunted by the ghost of George, the son of the former landlord. However, in the words of the fighter's wife, George always proved to be a friendly ghost.

The Noah's Ark, Tipton, has a long history of being haunted

Walsall (W. Mids)

Bentley Lane. In 1973, a young man travelling home in the early hours of the morning, found his car grinding to a halt with something invisible banging on the windscreen. The same thing happened to another young man in 1997.

Strangely enough, both men felt they had been saved from impending accidents which had actually happened further on down the lane.

A very young author sits on the car his friend had a strange experience with in Bentley Lane, Walsall, in the 70's

Walsall Town Hall has ghosts say staff from the curator's office, both past and present, who have been witness to a ghostly grey form that moves across the stage and middle of the hall and feel it may be the ghost of the wife of a former curator.

Walsall. site of the old Bentley Hall where several reports of a haunting by a spectral cavalier have been made. There has also been reports of strange noises.

crying and of a riderless black horse seen in the area in the early hours of the morning and at dusk.

Walsall, the Manor Hospital in Moat Street has lots of ghosts and funny "goings-on" including the ghost of the grumpy old matron and a very pretty nurse! The more unusual ones include a ghostly ambulance, strange bangs and noises, things being moved without explanation and old-time nurses in period dress putting in, well what can you say, unpaid service.

The White Hart Inn at Caldmore Green, is said to be the site of hauntings of several kinds over many years. Unfortunately, it had been badly damaged by fire some time ago but thankfully it has now been beautifully restored as a heritage centre and flats.

The beautifully rebuilt and refurbished White Hart, Caldmore Green, Walsall

Of course fire cannot hurt ghosts and there were at one time allegedly, quite a few to consider, such as a female servant and background to the so-called "Hand of Glory", a withered arm, which is actually still in the possession of Walsall

Library, and a story of a strange sword that was found there at some time. Before its restoration I visited the White Hart myself several times and without doubt it could only be described as strange!

The Hand of Glory displayed at Walsall Library, a gory find of the famous White Hart

June, a very down-to-earth lady, used to live on the Beechdale Estate in Walsall which at that time was quite a new council house. She had a large collection of Sixties-type records, The Beatles, Hollies and similar artists that she would play on the Dancette record player she owned. She also had copy of a record by Elvis Presley called Love Me Tender. Nothing strange about that except whenever she loaded up the automatic mechanism it would always drop several records at the same time but with uncanny regularity would always drop at and play Elvis' song. A few years later she met a lady who had lived at this house before her. June said nothing of her experience with the record player but apparently this lady's late son had been a very big fan of Elvis Presley and collected all his records and all sorts of memorabilia to do with him. Could there have been a connection? As they say, anything is possible.

50

The author in his young star-gazing days!

Lots of people claim they have seen the ghost of Elvis. The writer of this book hasn't, but he did stand under this statue in an unlikely setting outside a restaurant in Israel

Skulls are thought of as spooky at the best of times. This collection was photographed in Malta

Even telephone boxes it seems have their phantoms

The old Enville Rectory, Staffordshire, extras included on extreme right-hand side

The Whittington Inn. Was this at one time the
visiting place of Dick Turpin? Is it still!?

Something stirring in the deep waters?

53

Warwickshire

Astley Castle in Warwickshire, is said to be haunted by none other than Lady Jane Grey and her father, Lord Henry Grey, Duke of Suffolk. It is also haunted by the cowled figure of a monk who regularly walks the site at night - stopping, moving along and then peering at something apparent to him alone.

Warwick Castle is well worth a visit for all who are interested in ghosts. You may meet Moll Bloxham who is alleged to haunt the castle in the form of a big black dog, or the ghost of Sir Fulke Greville perhaps, who owned the castle in 1620. They also have a tower where screams, moans and all sorts of unexplained happenings are said to occur and it is indeed perhaps one of the most eerie sites you might ever visit.

Warwick Castle which has ghosts a-plenty!

Meon Hill, Warwickshire, can certainly be a quite unnerving and scary place, especially on dark nights. Perhaps we shouldn't be surprised really for this is an area of Warwickshire that in the distant past was believed to be where pagan crafts were practiced and I am led to believe that Meon Hill was especially linked to these practices. Correspondent, Tony Maplin, had quite a scary experience there one evening when he heard unearthly screams and right in front of him stood a huge black dog with a diamond-studded collar that seemed to glow in the dark. Meon Hill I believe is also a place where murder has taken place and that awful act, in my experience, can cause hauntings and the like especially where the case is never solved. There are also reports of hooded monks, a woman who carries her head under her arm and the sounds of swords on shields that clash in the night. A very strange place indeed.

Meriden. The Bull's Head public house in Meriden, is said to be haunted with the ghost of Frederick, a former waiter and employee of the old inn, who has been known to spill your drink for you!

The road from Leek Wootton to Warwick seems to have a long history of funny goings-on and many people have described visions that can only be described as one thing - Ghosts! Several people have seen horses and riders ride up the side of Blacklow Hill and then at the very top of the hill simply vanish without account. Could it have something to do with the execution of Piers Gaveston, special friend of Edward II who was taken this route before his execution in 1312 for what some claim to be unfair claims of perjury and deceit against several barons and noblemen. Indeed, many people over the years have reported seeing processions of noble horsemen and riders in between this area of Warwick Castle and Blacklow Hill, including a black horse and headless rider. Could it be Gaveston, perhaps remounting his horse, headless forever, trying to ride back and alter the awful fate of having his head removed from his body?

Warwickshire, Ragley Hall has a very long standing history of being haunted, one of the better known spectres being the so-called Lady in White.

Warwickshire, The Coventry to Rugby road. A large lorry with lights dimmed, hurtles down the wrong side of the carriageway then disappears upon an imminent collision.

Babbington Rectory, Warwickshire, has a history of hauntings that go back quite a few years and tales are told of a man in top hat, tails and carrying a stick that appears in and around the vicinity. Also a grey lady whom some say has not only appeared to them but also left behind the sweet smelling fragrance of her perfume.

Newdigate Colliery Warwickshire, had according to many miners a history of being haunted and those that took picks to the coal face tell tales of a large dark man in baggy trousers swinging a miner's lamp who could be two things, either very helpful or intent on scaring the living wits out of those that saw him, with not very much in between! The pit, at the best of times can be a dark dreary place to work in and only the toughest of men can do the job, but like my own great grandfather would say, when you're deep underground lad, anything can happen and some things you will never understand, go on there.

The Abbeygate, Coombe Abbey, Warwickshire has many ghosts according to Susan Daley and she should know because she has investigated the building herself. Perhaps the most famous is a gentleman called Abbot Geoffrey, put to death by a fellow monk many years ago and apparently now locked forever more into finding out the reason why. Some say he is to blame when glasses and other objects are unexplainably broken or crash against a wall. Sensitives and psychics seem to think his presence is in the old cloisters. There is also the story of a beautiful young girl with jet black hair and flashing eyes who is sometimes seen happy and gay but at other times is seen weeping and wringing her hands in sorrow. I am also told that the sound of horses hooves and unearthly screams have also been heard. There are also elements that suggest the surrounding areas could well be one of those areas that experience time-slip that I have spoken of in other parts of my book. Yes, a very interesting area indeed.

Warwickshire, Shuckburgh Hall is said to be haunted by Lieutenant Sharp who during the last century fell in love with the daughter of the manor who absolutely forbade their relationship to continue. Lieutenant Sharp could not live without his lady and in a desperate act first shot the girl and then himself. Ever since there are those that say that they have both seen them arm in arm as a couple and individually. Others have heard gunshots that have no earthly source to the present time.

Wednesbury (W. Mids)

Wednesbury, numerous reports of a ghostly brown dog that roams the King's Hill area of the town and usually brings a warning of some nature to the people who see it.

Wednesfield (W. Mids)

Wednesfield. Lynn Smith told me about quite a funny ghost story really. Some years ago she was walking with her friend Carol near to the New Cross Hospital, when they walked past two young men leaning against a wall eating fish and chips. One of the boys wolf-whistled the girls, the other called them back and asked them if they would like some chips. Both girls pretended not to hear them but whispered to each other that they were rather nice with a remark that one of them looked very much like Billy Fury, a top pop star at that time. Carol insisted she wanted to speak to them so both girls, not wishing to appear forward, crossed the road using it as an excuse to walk back past them hoping the boys would notice them, but they were no longer there. In the blinking of an eye or the time it took the girls to turn round and cross the road, no more than thirty or forty feet in front of them, they had quite simply vanished into thin air and had taken their fish and chips with them!

Wednesfield has a haunted telephone box right in the high street according to Sue Jackson who had a very strange experience there twice in 1997. On her way to work one morning she realised she had forgotten to make her husband's sandwiches for work that day, her husband being on a two-to-ten shift working system, so she stopped at the phone box to make a call. The phone rang and after three rings it answered and a voice said, "I'm sorry Susan's not here right now." Nothing unusual about that you might say, except Sue is absolutely sure it was the voice of her Grandma who had been dead for over four years. She dropped the phone and drove straight home. Her husband was still in bed and insisted the phone had never even rung. Puzzled, but not a person who really believed in that sort of thing, to use her words, she just went on to work and forgot it, but it must have played on her mind to some extent because on her return journey she decided to stop at the box again. She went in, picked up the phone and rang her home number, knowing at this time of the evening there would be no one at home. The phone rang three times then was answered with, "I'm sorry, but Susan's not here right now."

Wellington (Shrops)

Wellington, Overley Hall is haunted by several ghosts, one being a small girl of the Victorian period who seems to skip along the ground in a very dainty manner then simply vanishes into thin air.

West Bromwich (W. Mids)

John South wrote to me about a very interesting experience he had recently outside West Bromwich Library, in broad daylight and at about midday. He was on his way to the library to collect some books and right outside the building he saw an immaculate dusky pink Ford Consul of the late Fifties and more unusual, just behind it, a jet black Vauxhall Cresta or maybe Velox with very unusual orange headlights. It has to be said that John was very interested in cars of the late Fifties and early Sixties, so immediately moved over to have a closer look at what to him were two very attractive cars but as he did so they simply seemed to dissolve and vanished from sight before his very eyes. He was quite sure he did not imagine this vision and quoting John, it was a little too early for a drink that day, so is it possible that he slipped into a Fifties or early Sixties time-slip? Does anyone actually remember parking those two cars specifically together outside the building at that specific time in history? Now that would be an interesting example of time slip or ghostly repeated event!

Sandwell General Hospital. Several of the nurses tell me stories of having quite scary experiences on occasions. One of the wards is apparently haunted by a male figure who has allegedly actually pinned some of the nurses down during their rest period whilst on the night-shift. Does he object to them having a catnap? Some of the nurses have also spoken of the sound of strange, haunting music that even more unusually seems to be playing backwards. Of course almost every hospital has its share of ghosts, but this one is particularly strange and so far unexplainable, though reported by too many of the staff to be put down to a tall tale.

Willenhall (W. Mids)

Willenhall. Behind Temple Road is an area of rural, rough land the locals know as The Summers. It was here that one of my correspondents, Mr Capewell, saw strange glowing lights on more than one occasion when he lived in the area. locals tell me it is the ghosts of Cholera victims buried there many years ago when Willenhall was blighted with this awful sickness, but I have found no evidence at all to support this opinion. Could it be the result of rising gases? I asked this but other people have told me they have seen strange, misty substances that seem to move in and around the area of The Summers on certain nights of the year.

Willenhall, Bell Alley is situated right next door to the old Bell Inn. This is allegedly where the ghost of a young girl who had actually been murdered many years ago is said to walk. She has been seen on her own and with her mother, who is reputed to have committed suicide upon finding the poor little girl murdered by one of her own men friends.

An artist's impression of what the little alley wench and her mother of Willenhall could have looked like

Additions New Age shop, Walsall Road, had a very strange experience reported to me by Tony Ball, who saw a glowing light all around a picture on one of the walls. Proprietor, Sue Addis, confirmed Tony's story, having seen this herself and having customers point to the glowing light and asking for an explanation, in this very pleasant and friendly shop.

The site of the old churchyard near Wood Street, was where a young man in the Seventies saw a very strange vision of perfectly formed man with a bear's head, which apparently stopped the young lads playing around this area - could this have been the reason for his appearance? Also, in the Seventies two young men, Phil and Rob, saw a very tall, dark figure that seemed to float several feet off the floor and caused both young men to leave Wood Street in a hurry!

Wellington Villa at one time stood on the corner of Walsall Road and the Bilston Road. Several correspondents who actually lived there at one time all say it was one of the most haunted houses in Willenhall. Ghosts included a very tall man in dark dress and top hat carrying a black silver-topped stick. I actually saw him myself as a boy. Others spoke of hearing the ghostly sound of horses long-since gone in the stables at the rear of the house. The site is now occupied by a large commercial van sales lot. I wonder if the tall dark gentleman is ever seen there now?

Mr Walton, one of my correspondents, told me of a most interesting unexplained occurrences that happened to several people who had worked at the British Road Service haulage company in Gipsy Lane, Willenhall. Late at night and, strangely, especially on foggy evenings, some people claimed they could hear Rock'n'Roll of the Fifties being played, loud motorcycles revving up and the laughter and voices of teenagers from no apparent source. For security reasons this sort of thing had to be investigated thoroughly but no one could ever find out where the sounds were coming from. Perhaps even stranger still, one driver even saw two Teddy Boys dressed in brightly coloured jackets and crepe soled shoes walk past the BRS, up into Gipsy Lane and vanished before his very eyes. When told of this story, it was particularly interesting to me for at one time my own father promoted such events at a building called the Toc 'H' Club which had been right next door to the BRS. Could this be significant? Were the people at the company, sensitives if you like, seeing a time-slip experience? It may be that I actually know the answer to that but you will have to read about it in another book in the future.

Willenhall, a local author I know very well, in 1990 was writing a new book and late one night was dictating information to a tape recorder, when he fell asleep and left the machine running. The next day he played the tape back. Everything was blank except for one voice in a Cockney accent saying, "Oh my Gawd!" My friend played it back to a neighbour who, both excited and agitated exclaimed, "That's the man who used to live in your bungalow, but he's dead! Must have been about thirty years ago I should think."

Wolverhampton (W. Mids)

Wolverhampton, there have been reports of horses that inexplicably appear, galloping down Steelhouse Lane before suddenly disappearing into thin air.

Moseley Old Hall is a very strange building, a place I have visited when completely empty, on my own, and with family and friends. According to the guides it is not haunted, but I certainly felt it was, especially in the upper area of the building. Subsequently I have received letters from several people including a very good medium called Beryl Davies, who, like me, confirmed she certainly sensed a presence on the top floor of the hall. I have also received several letters from different people who say they have seen cavaliers and roundheads in the vicinity of this building. Another letter from a Mrs Jones of Wolverhampton told me of a gathering of monks who walked in procession tolling a bell. Her husband could not see the figures but claims he heard the bell.

Beacon/WABC Radio Station in Tettenhall. I am informed that the radio station has a history of being haunted. Apparently at one time the building had been an orphanage and in the area that had formerly been the old chapel is the site where the vision of a little girl has been seen sitting by a fireside and also in a chair. There is also the story of an older lady who is seen carrying a tray up the stairs and once one of the presenters saw a vision standing right in front of the photocopier, but apparently this is just a few of the strange things that happen here.

Wolverhampton Central Library is said to have a ghost that staff sense whenever they alter things or try to change things around so to speak, especially putting books in new areas will lead to books that inexplicably fall off shelves, the sense of someone standing behind you or even tapping your shoulder or the sound of a faint "Tut! Tut! Tut!" Could it be that the old gentleman, as some staff have described him, feels everything should remain as it was in his day? It is one possibility isn't it?

The bridge at Neachell's Lane in the early seventies was where two youths, Phil and Les, who at that time worked at the nearby Decca factory, saw what they could only describe as something that looked like a goblin or very ugly dwarf who ran across the bridge onto the nearby rough fields and completely vanished.

Civic Hall, Wolverhampton, much of the spooky goings-on happen in the Wulfruna Hall's so-called Green Room which archivists discovered was built exactly where the old Wolverhampton morgue once stood. A strange occurrence happened one evening when top rock band Gun were appearing and their lighting operator was alone in the gallery and repeatedly found someone or something tapping him on the shoulder. He left the gallery half way through the concert and told the Civic Manager, Mark Blackstock, "There's no way I'm going back up there!" and never did. According to Mr Blackstock other members of his staff have also been tapped on the shoulder, shadows have come from a cupboard and the cleaners have reported strange odours and perfumes. A figure has also been seen on stage at both the Wulfruna and the Main Civic Halls that can only be described as ghostly. Indeed, several years ago in the company of friends, I also saw a ghostly figure on stage at the same time that local pop band Slade were playing. A most haunted place indeed is the Civic Hall.

The BBC Radio Studios in Queen Street have strange goings-on, unexplained noises, loud bangs and voices have all been heard in the past. Two of the DJ's, Gary and Des, together with Pete Whitehouse, chairman of Wolverhampton Community Radio, all of whom I know well, all describe the top-floor studio as being strange at certain times, especially at night.

Wrottesley Road, Tettenhall near Wolverhampton, has a very large old house which, according to Steve Powell who worked there for several years, was at one time haunted by the white smoky outline of the head and shoulders of an elderly lady who would peer from one of the windows of the old house. According to Mr Powell some information suggests the lady may have worked there at some time and was most likely to put in an appearance in the month of July.

Wolverhampton, the magnificent Grand Theatre is where the ghost or presence of Mr Purdey, a friendly former manager is very often seen and the sweet perfume of a lady in grey. One member of staff also told me that in the bar area glasses get moved, people get tapped on the shoulder and the old-fashioned fragrance of lavender has been known to waft in and around the area. Numerous artists who have known nothing of these ghosts have described exactly what I have outlined for you.

The Grand Theatre, Wolverhampton, apparently has its ghosts, but then almost every theatre in England has its share of phantoms and spectres

Wolverley (Worcs)

Wolverley, Sebright School in the early 1950's had been the home of one of my correspondents, Jean Hart, whose father worked as a gardener and caretaker at Buryhall House. Her mother often heard footsteps in the passages that led from room to room and her father once saw a handle turn and the door open without anyone being there. Eventually an Irish lady, the cook, who had been at the school for many years told this story to them. Apparently a few years before another gardener and his wife together with another couple who were not married had a little too much to drink and the men retired to one room and the women to another but, unfortunately, a tragedy was to occur. The gas had been left on and although Jean explained the full story to me in a letter, to cut a long story short, they all lost their lives that evening. After hearing this story the family were never worried further and afterwards often said goodnight to what they thought was the ghost they called William and never had any real trouble from him. Apparently, the gardener's house where the family lived is now gone and has been turned into other buildings and in Jean's words, she doesn't even know if William is still there. It just goes to show that sometimes being scared of ghosts is just not understanding what they are or what causes them.

Wombourne (Staffs)

A few years ago a Wombourne family showed me a very interesting photograph of which I have a copy in my private collection. It is of a gravestone at a local church which clearly shows a smiling face on it. Even stranger is that the family are quite certain it is the late elder sister of a young bride and the photograph had actually been taken on the very day of her wedding.

Worcestershire

Worcestershire, the village of Broadway. It is stated that during the Reformation the good church people of Broadway hid their church bells in Middle Hill Beech Wood to save them from being looted. Yet there are those that claim they have heard the bells ringing at dusk and late at night and have clearly heard clanging during the First and, indeed, Second World War, when the ringing of bells was certainly not allowed.

Callow End at Priors Court, is a very interesting place and is reputed to have several ghosts including a Civil War soldier and a young girl seen in and around the courtyard. This ghost was actually seen by my own father whilst completing part of his military service during the Second World War.

Besford Court, Worcestershire, is haunted by a lady in grey, some say when its sole use was as a great house. The upstairs rooms could be strange at times.

Chapter Two

The A to Z of Ghosts

A - Animals - The Ghosts of a great many animals have been reported throughout the years. Dogs, especially black ones, cats and horses are the most numerous

B - Banshee - the legend of the Banshee originally came from Scotland and Ireland and was always a woman sometimes old but sometimes young who was said to appear wailing at the home of her ancestors indicating a death was imminent. People have described them as having very long hair and red piercing eyes.

B - Bogey Man - It is a very well known expression if you are not good the Bogey Man will get you! and has been used for many a long year to make naughty boys and girls behave themselves but once was believed that the Bogey Man was one of the most evil and powerful of ghosts because he was the assistant of Satan and the intentions to make men do bad things on Earth. It was claimed the Bogey Man could also change his shape and appearance but more often than not would be very dark, thick set and often very hairy with an awful grinning face. People of Celtic origin believed the Bogey Man could be driven away by holding up the Bible in front of them.

C - Crossroads - Crossroads have always been places throughout history where ghosts appear to be seen time and time again. An old legend in the Black Country says that ghosts often appear at crossroads because this is a place where many people would have met in the past and the links of friendship draw them back time and time again.

D - Doppelganger - The word Doppelganger originates from Germany and it is one of the strangest of ghosts for in truth it is the ghost of someone who is actually still alive. I have personally investigated many instances of doppelganger experiences.

E - Ectoplasm - Some very talented mediums usually called physical mediums produce ectoplasm which usually appears as a cloudy liquid substance from the head of the medium and from this ectoplasm spirits are often seen and formed.

F - Fairy Folk - Are fairies real or folklore? It is a question put to me by many people and my answer is that for sure many people that I respect claim that they have seen or have known of the existence of fairies. Even the great Sir Arthur Conan Doyle despite publication of photographs by two young girls who later retracted their evidence continued in his belief.

G - Ghouls - The origin of the ghoul is said to come from the deserts of Arabia where it appeared to travelling nomads with a horrible scary face. The ghoul is believed to have a taste for human flesh and legend says that it stole dead bodies and devoured them. No wonder the legend of the ghoul is a very frightening ghost indeed.

G - Gremlins - A gremlin is one of the most newly talked of spectres and no doubt has much to do with the popular films about them. But the real ones were seen and talked about by the pilots of the Second World War who claimed to have seen these ugly, dwarf-like creatures in different parts of their planes even on the wings as they flew them with the intentions generally of causing problems. However, my research has indicated that many pilots actually thought they were there to help them and look after them. Today they are reported in garages and factories, perhaps it is machines and engines that draws them.

H - Headless Ghosts - For centuries we have read stories about ghosts without heads or those from history that carry them under their arm. Many stories surround the wives of Henry the Eighth of England and I suppose it is not surprising really. In life for sure some of his wives had their heads separated from their bodies, but in my experience most ghosts are seen in totality.

I - Incubus - Legend says that this was the spirit of a beautiful young girl who would appear and take on the physical form to seduce as many young men as possible leaving them forever enchanted by their charms. Succubus is the male equivalent.

J - Jack O'Lanterns - These ghosts apparently are seen as small glowing balls of light said to shine when someone has passed away or is about to die. Other legends say that they are there to attract and draw you into difficult places and they are often seen where there are swamps, bogs and dangerous conditions. They are, however, said to have an attraction that fatally lures you towards them even when aware of the dangers.

K - Kelpie - Kelpie is really a ghost of Scotland who is said to always appear close to water. A kelpie is sometimes a most attractive young man but more generally a handsome horse who will often accommodatingly allow you to ride him, then dash away before throwing you into the nearest river, lake or pool.

L - Lights - Throughout history men and women have seen lights that they have associated with spirits and ghosts. It is often said combinations of glowing balls of light represent spirit formations though in a not so pleasant context for seafaring folk often claimed that unexplainable lights have drawn them onto rocks where they have been shipwrecked for no apparent reason.

M - Materialisation - The most popular form of materialisation in the early 1900's was the production of ectoplasm from different parts of the body. Today when we speak of materialisation it is generally the seeing clearly of a ghost or spirit in materialised form.

N - Nixies - Nixies are generally seen and spoken of as German water spirits and are often described as having a human body and their lower limbs like a fish and are often mistaken for mermaids. However, legend has suggested that they are not so kind as a traditional mermaid and have often been known to lure humans to watery deaths.

O - Oriental Ghosts - Ghosts from Japan and China are of some of the most unusual. Chinese ghosts are often chinless yet speak and are said to bring wisdom. Japanese ghosts often appear as Samurai warriors. Lady Japanese ghosts are said to be beautiful women who can easily change into foxes and bewitch mortal men with their cunning and beauty.

P - Poltergeists - A poltergeist is not a pleasant ghost for it generally causes lots of problems like loud noises and bangs and moving around of large objects and can be scary for some people. Almost always in my experience poltergeist activity occurs where there is a young teenager in the house passing through puberty and as soon as the teenager passes through this phase in their life or, indeed, the case is investigated, everything often comes to an end. Poltergeist activity can be very unpleasant for those suffering its inconvenience.

R - Revenants - Quite wrongly revenants are often seen as simply another name for a ghost. What it actually means is someone who returned from the dead even after quite some time often appearing in the clothes they most often wore in life.

There have even been reports of groups of soldiers and warriors reappearing in the areas they occupied centuries after their death in full military or tribal battle dress.

S - Spook - Spooks are often ghosts specifically talked about in America and it is understood they were spoken of by the native American Indians who believed these ghosts could take control of their living bodies. In the past many Americans actually believed that these types of spooks could help them achieve great material success and consciously assist them with their ventures.

V - Vampires - Legends of vampire ghosts do exist but are not really to be associated with Bram Stoker's story of Dracula but more in India where spirits known as viricas are said to roam about at night making awful chattering noises as they search for the opportunity of drinking human blood. Some Indians in rural parts of the country leave offerings of food to sustain the virakas in the hope they will leave them and theirs alone.

W - White Ladies - The ghosts of white ladies are found pretty well all over the world but most commonly in castles, manor houses and similar types of buildings. They are often ladies of an aristocratic type background royals or the wives of great noblemen.

W - Wraiths - This is not really a ghost but generally a vision of someone who is still alive. Legend does suggest that the appearance of this vision often indicate the forthcoming death of the person whose vision is seen but as we have learned more about astral projection and travel this is not always the case and perfectly well people are often seen in this way by others.

Z - Zombie - There are legends that say by use of magic there have been people with the ability to bring back life into a corpse by allowing a spirit to re-enter the body for a short while operating that body almost like a robot with no will of its own. The legend probably originates from the West Indies and has certainly been the major topic of many horror films in the West in recent years.

Chapter Three

A Toolkit For Ghost Hunters
(including new technology equipment and photography)

This is what you will need for a very basic toolkit to investigate ghosts. Later on in the chapter I will tell you of some of the very latest technology equipment that is getting ever closer to definitely proving their existence.

1. Notepad
2. Pen and Pencil
3. Retractable ruler
4. 12" ruler
5. Watch - digital, nightlight
6. A good magnifying glass
7. Spool of black cotton
8. String
9. Tape recorder
10. Contact Adhesive - 1" tape
11. Powerful torch
12. A good thermometer
13. Packet of chalks
14. Talcum powder and 1" paintbrush
15. Pencil sharpener
16. Camera - built-in powerful flash
17. Video camera
18. Spare batteries for everything!

A notepad and pens and pencils are vital for making notes of anything that happens. Note exactly and absolutely factually any occurrences or sounds that are heard. Also note whether they were witnessed by someone else apart from you. Time and date them precisely. You will find the magnifying glass that I have included in your kit of immeasurable use when looking at footprints and handprints. They may be invisible to the human eye but you will see them through your glass. It can also be used for examining traces of post-ghostly substances left behind.

Hello! Hello! Hello! What's this then?

The talcum powder and the paintbrush can also be very useful in conjunction with the magnifying glass. For example, if you shake the talc onto a cupboard, a chair, or perhaps a table or anything with a polished surface, then gently blow it away, it will leave impressions of prints, natural or supernatural, that are there. Now should that print or prints not match any of those of the residents or visitors, you've got your first winner. You're learning the tricks of the trade of ghost hunting!

Now let's move to your chalks - you can use them to mark around movable objects such as chairs or table legs which have perhaps been reported to move around on their own. It may involve a long sitting on your part but if you have chalked it and it moves, you've got another winner, haven't you?

The string, self-adhesive tape and cotton are for securing and sealing doors and windows. Far and away the best of the three, in my opinion, is the self-adhesive tape. For example, use about four or five pieces cut at about three inches and place them on the doors and frames which are reported as self-opening; set up your watch; the evidence of any breakage of the tape will be obvious.

A tape-recorder is also a most useful tool for anyone researching the existence of ghosts and should accompany you on every enquiry if at all possible. I would also suggest that you buy some extra batteries for it - the type that can be recharged time and time again. (Actually you should always carry a spare set of batteries for everything). They are an excellent investment and I do suggest that your tape-recorder should be on record at all times. However, be on your guard for there is usually a natural explanation for most sounds.

Investing in a good camera is absolutely vital. I stress good rather than expensive and the fewer requirements for adjustments of controls the better. It should incorporate an infra-red focus lock if at all possible and at the time of writing this article, the type of camera I have described can be purchased for less than a hundred pounds. This is indeed the simple type of camera I use, and I find the infra-red lock and built-in flash invaluable at night. A video camera is also an excellent piece of equipment to take on any investigation with you, but I do suggest that you explain to the supplier exactly what you want to use it for, some video cameras in my experience are much better than others for filming in the dark and it is best not to be tempted into buying a video camera with lots of features, things to set, etc. Basically, if you see a ghost, you want to point and shoot immediately, so keep it simple.

I shall now move onto the thermometer. This is absolutely essential, as temperatures often drop alarmingly just before, during and for a short period after supernatural happenings, psychic manifestations and, of course, anywhere with a so-called cold spot is always of interest so you do need a good thermometer really and you should check it often. Keep a record of any temperature changes and record them precisely.

Obviously, this is a very basic ghost hunter's kit that I have outlined for you, and expensive equipment (if you can afford it) might prove more successful. Such equipment might include highly advanced video cameras, closed-circuit TV, infra-red telescopes, volt meters and possibly highly technical equipment that can detect humidity and electro-magnetic field changes. However, and I am sure to offend some of my colleagues here, in my opinion, most of the better evidence that has been found comes from very good amateurs using the type of kit I have recommended for you in this article, on numerous broadcasts that I have made and in one of my books, Ghosts of the Midlands and How to Detect Them. But at the end of the day I suppose it comes down to what you want to use. Try to invent new gadgets that you can make use of yourself and never be afraid to experiment with your efforts to prove the existence of ghosts.

At this stage, let me be very frank with you, investigating paranormal activity can be tremendously exhilarating and exciting. However, it can also be tremendously boring at times, when hour after hour passes with nothing at all being seen or heard. Suddenly you hear a noise which proves to be nothing more than the friendly cat of the house, or a chilling wind is found to come from the air-brick behind the cupboard, and I would advise all those tracking down ghosts to remember that you should look for the natural answer before hypothesising the supernatural. However, as with another activity that I am quite interested in - angling - you will often sit for hours and hours waiting for that one bite. You have got to be patient and dedicated because you will find evidence or see something in the end - of that you can be sure.

Always remember the simple things like tape recorder and torch

Earlier in this chapter I have told you all about the ghost hunter's kit - the simple things that almost anyone can get together and get out there to try to see ghosts for yourself. But if you are really serious about the subject and you've got the money to spare we now have some very special new technology equipment that is used by professional paranormal investigators and for sure would give you a real edge in proving ghosts do exist.

Really genuine scientific appliances were first used by the Society for

Psychical Research well over one hundred years ago and properly controlled experiments alongside photography were being used. Unfortunately, for the next hundred years things did not move on very much and those that wished to make detached investigations of the paranormal and ghosts had to rely on the stories that people told them and the support of people like myself, psychics and mediums. By and large I am sure these investigations were generally conducted and taken forward in a professional manner but would always leave us open to the accusation, "Where is your real hard evidence?" Of course some basic scientific tools for the job were brought into use, especially film and recording equipment but the bulkiness of their size and great cost made them unobtainable and prohibitive and only for the very serious ghost detectives and hunters. However, in the mid-eighties things really changed and amazing progress was made in computer and microchip technology. Alongside this fact prices tumbled down to remarkably cheap levels that has made them available to the man in the street and semi-professionals. Equipment came onto the market that could detect and record environmental changes aimed mostly for use by the medical profession and the electronics industry.

However, ghost hunters and those interested in investigating the paranormal quickly realised they could ideally be used on their ghost hunts and general investigations of paranormal phenomena. In simple terms this equipment could be used to detect changes or recognise interactions with physical environment as we understand it and without a shadow of a doubt in the Nineties experimenting with this type of equipment has shown altered states and interactions can be recorded where ghosts and hauntings are taking place.

Of course, at this stage we have not actually come up with what could positively be called a ghost detecting piece of equipment. Perhaps before we can do that we will have to definitely and positively be able to say what a ghost is as I have explained to you in other parts of this book. However, equipment is now there if you can afford to buy it at what, remember, are now very reasonable prices, which can detect and show, well how can I put it, that a ghostly presence or some sort of haunting experience is going on. The type of equipment that I am talking about are the electromagnetic field meters which are capable of giving irregular electromagnetic field readings in places where ghosts have been seen or are sensed. Of course, it must be remembered that there are all sorts of magnetic readings that can be picked up by your meter from electrical appliances, such as television sets, radios, underground electric wiring, overhead wiring and all sorts of other similar objects, therefore, you have to locate these energy sources and eliminate them from your investigation.

Unexplainable electromagnetic fields should be unquestionably not relevant to any of the things I have just mentioned, constantly change, intensify and weaken and show movement from one place to another. Experience suggests they are often found in areas that perfectly match where a good medium or psychic has described the presence of a spirit, ghost or other psychic phenomenon. An inexpensive piece of equipment called a magnetometer is used by many ghost hunters and investigators of the paranormal generally. The influence of electromagnetic fields has been known to change and distort sound and produce strange voice sound recordings on audio tape. Electromagnetic fields also affect video tape recording, which often shows up as misty or unclear images, sometimes figure-like. Today, you may also find the modern ghost hunter using a radiation meter to see if there are higher than normal levels of gamma radiation present as some investigators of the paranormal have suggested. Geiger counters have been used to test and sense high levels of ionising radiation where mediums and psychics have seen or sensed ghosts.

Ghost hunters have always been very interested in cold spots and have always associated these areas with ghosts. A very useful piece of equipment now available is a quick reacting electronic thermometer (this is nothing like the old ones filled with alcohol for taking room temperatures and is far more accurate). A good quality one will remain quite steady at its room reading temperature ability and be equipped with a probe that can be placed in and respond to any cold spots. The best of this equipment records ongoing data and can be even set up to buzz or give an alarm signal when temperatures significantly drop or rise above set standard patterns. For quite a while we have had nightscopes and today, organisations such as the police force and army have special light intensifying binoculars for surveillance at night. Unfortunately, this equipment does not work in the pitch dark but does automatically and electronically recognise levels of available light such as that provided by the moon, whereby a reasonable image which could not be seen with ordinary vision or photograph is possible. I am sure I do not need to explain to any would be ghost hunters out there what a tremendous opportunity this type of equipment offers for all night surveillance of an alleged haunted building which could have all its lights switched off and no light playing upon it. I would have to say to you, however, that I am not convinced ghosts only appear at night, indeed I am quite sure they are equally active during daylight hours but the advantages of such a piece of equipment in investigating the traditional night time ghost is obvious to all I would have thought and some experts insist ghosts do only appear at night and that both sunlight and artificial light is prohibitive to them putting in an appearance, so to speak!

Author looking at a local farm at dusk using nightscopes

The last piece of equipment and perhaps the most important are thermal imaging cameras which have been made great use of in the medical profession for several years and show up images very clearly relevant to the heat they give out. Ghost hunters first put thermal cameras to use to take pictures of cold spots that throughout history have been sensed and felt by mediums and psychics and ordinary everyday people, in places they felt something strange was going on. In the last few years ghost hunters and the like have also become interested in hot spots and thermal imaging cameras can also be used in the appropriate way here. Strangely, the centre of these hotspots is often very cold. It would have to be said of course that thermal imaging cameras, really good ones that is, are still far too expensive for the ordinary ghost hunter or researcher of the paranormal. However, when radio stations, TV companies and very large newspapers get to know you it is sometimes possible to get them to hire them for you or borrow them if you can link them into an interesting feature or story. Black and white thermal imaging cameras are much cheaper and sometimes outdated equipment is offered at a bargain price from organisations such as the fire brigade or police force, but in truth experience seems to suggest that they are neither completely sensitive enough or really applicable for the investigation of ghosts or paranormal activity. Having said that, a few years ago I am sure I would have been highly delighted to get my hands on such equipment so don't turn it down if you can get it for a bargain price.

As I said right at the start of this chapter we do not really have an exact appliance that will positively say yes this is a ghost but there again we don't exactly know what a ghost is for sure, but we do now have equipment that can show and detect unexplainable changes and its advantages in a haunted house are obvious. Undoubtedly, during the last twenty-five years we have made amazing advancement and progress in developing equipment that will ultimately give us the ability in the future, I hope, to say, yes, here categorically, we do have a ghost.

Time and time again people have said to me that if ghosts exist how come we never see photographs of them always stating that if they could see a photograph of a ghost then they would believe in them. They are usually surprised when I tell them there are many, many photographs of ghosts taken over the years which are claimed to be real ghosts and despite professional investigation have not been disproved. I have several photographs of ghosts taken by myself and others and are undoubtedly very interesting and are certainly not fakes. However, in the past and particularly in the early days of the popularity of spiritualism in this country many fake photographs were passed off as the real thing, double exposures being a favourite. These basically are two pictures taken on the same frame. Another old favourite was to place the ghostly spectre on the negative as it was being printed or developed. I can assure you I do have pictures which are not in my opinion fakes but equally I hope I am sensible enough to realise that there have been many fakes in the past and with the advancement of photography today it is much easier to produce pictures that just aren't what they seem. Equally, now we know so much more about photography our expert colleagues cannot be taken in so easily.

Most people who are interested in seeing pictures of ghosts today use a video camera and of course there can be great difficulties and accusations of cheating with this sort of equipment for it is so easy to arrange for someone or something to appear on film that would make the general public think here is that special picture or piece of film that we have all been looking for. Another problem is that whatever ghosts are, quite a lot of them seem incapable of being reproduced in pictures and on film and as I have said in other parts of this book, so many different types of ghosts exist - is it that surprising really? But I also believe it is vitally important that we do continue to strive to produce evidence of pictures and films and if so-called experts always insist on ridiculing ninety-nine out of every hundred, that hundredth picture that they cannot disprove does help to prove the existence of ghosts and unexplained phenomena.

A hooded monk? Well no, not really - but the author really chilling out? Yes!

Chapter Four

Ghosts From Further Afield

Obviously, most of the stories and information I have told you about in this book relates to the English Midlands. But sometimes those of you that are really interested in the subject will want to travel a little further afield. In this chapter I will try to suggest to you a selection of places throughout the British Isles that might be of interest to you.

England

London - the whole of London really - is a very haunted area. Hampton Court, for instance, has many ghosts which include two of Henry VIII's wives, Catherine Howard and Jane Seymour, and there are those that say they have seen the lady known as Mistress Penn, governess of Jane and King Henry VIII's son, Edward, on several occasions in the south-west wing. Allegedly, there are at least another twenty or thirty unknown ghosts at Hampton Court that have at one time or another in history put in an appearance, to coin a phrase!

Drury Lane, it is said, you may see a vision of Nell with her basket of oranges but even more haunted is the Theatre Royal where a man in eighteenth century dress has been regularly seen. Could it be the spectre of someone who had been killed there many years before? Other stars of the stage have reported seeing the ghosts of actors and actresses no longer of this world, especially in the dressing room areas.

Westminster Abbey is also reportedly haunted and some claim to have seen the ghost of Charles II in the Deanery, although a ghost some people believe to be Father Benedictus, has been seen more frequently in the cloisters.

St Thomas's Hospital has several ghosts modern and old, these include the spectre of a young nurse who actually attends to some patients. Some claim to have even seen the ghost of the great Florence Nightingale.

Biggins Hill, a strange haunting because it is the sound of a Spitfire or Hurricane engine that is heard spluttering and misfiring at times and not the way they would generally be expected to sound, but is it because this is a badly damaged aircraft replaying its last flight home?

The area known as Marnhull in Wiltshire has a strange haunting. Two figures have been seen carrying a coffin. Some say the figures have no faces, others that they are partially hidden by hoods.

Not far from Beckhampton in Wiltshire is a site called the Highwayman's Grave, a robber was allegedly shot there by railway policemen, though gipsies have always claimed him as one of their own and innocent and for many years left flowers and tokens on the site.

A Gypsy Girl's Lost Love

Hinton Ampner in Hampshire is a very haunted building which has both male and female ghosts, doors that crash closed, moans and reports of crying and screaming have all apparently been heard. Some people believe that some of the ghosts include Lord Storwell and that of his sister-in-law with whom he allegedly had a liaison. Upon demolition of the old house a skull was found under the floorboards and many stories indeed have been told of Hinton Ampner Manor.

Bramber Castle in Sussex where the children of William de Breone died of imprisonment and malnutrition are seen by those with a sensitive gift, heartbreakingly begging for food in and around the areas of the castle.

Castle Hastings can be an unnerving building at times, groans, crying and the clanking of heavy chains have all been heard. There are several ghosts alleged to haunt this castle including Thomas a Becket and a lady in white.

Canterbury Cathedral is said to have more than its share of ghosts. Perhaps Thomas a Becket's death here has something to do with his alleged appearances.

Oxney Court in Kent is said to be haunted by a very beautiful lady that wears very dark clothes and has indeed been seen by many people. Some say she is so real in appearance that many who have seen her would have not even realised they were seeing a ghost!

Puttenden Manor in Surrey has had some strange phenomena over the years. Not only have strange figures been seen around the buildings, perfume and the aromatic burning of pipe tobacco have also been smelt by more than one person.

Avenbury Church in Herefordshire is a strange place where there are those that claim to have heard the sound of what can only be described as unearthly music and song.

Glastonbury, Somerset is a lovely place to visit with so many legends of King Arthur, the planting of the Thorn by Joseph of Arimathea and over the years many people have claimed they have seen various visions which include, I am told, monks, Druids and a Roundhead soldier, the abbey being a favourite site.

Althorp House apparently has several ghosts, one including an old servant who visits guests at night in a quite friendly sort of way apparently just to see that all is well. One can only wonder if Princess Diana ever saw this friendly lady.

Salisbury Hall in Hertfordshire has many ghosts including, allegedly, the Duke of St Albans, illegitimate child of Charles II and Nell Gwyn. The Churchill family also spent some time here and it is reported that some members of the family saw the ghosts of servants in old-type dress and one spectre they were quite sure was Nell Gwyn. There have also been reports of soldiers from the English Civil War. A very haunted house indeed apparently.

Camfield Place, Hertfordshire, is a most interesting haunting and was once both the residence of Beatrix Potter and Barbara Cartland. Reports have been passed on of candles that have been blown out on their own and of the ghosts of pets animals and other strange apparitions.

Rainham Hall in Essex is another well documented haunted house apparently still visited by Colonel Mulliner whom you are just as likely to see by day as you are by night.

Beeleigh Abbey, Essex, is a strange place and has its fair share of ghosts including monks, nuns and some say the ghost of Sir John Gates, put to death for his support of Lady Jane Grey's claim to the throne of England.

Sawston Hall, Cambridgeshire, is a very haunted house, some say by Mary Tudor who certainly played her part in having the building erected in the first place. There is also allegedly a white lady and reports of strange noises and the unexplained opening and closing of doors.

Blickling Hall in Norfolk has its fair share of ghosts including Ann Boleyn who lived there as a little girl. There are also reports of a ghostly coach and horses, strange noises and music.

Raynham Hall, Norfolk, has become a well documented building mainly because of the publication of one of the most famous photographs ever taken of a ghost, that of the so-called Brown Lady walking down the staircase at Raynham Hall.

Bosworth Hall, Leicestershire, has an unusual haunting feature - a red mark or stain that appears never to dry out. There are also reports of the appearance of a lady who had once been mistress of Bosworth Hall appearing in and around the building.

Nottingham Castle has a long history that says it is haunted and that one of its ghosts is Queen Isabella who walks the castle area in a constant, unending search for her lover.

Capesthorne Hall in Cheshire has ghosts. Shadowy figures have been seen in and around the chapel. There is also a legend of a hand or arm that opens doors and windows and also of a lady in white.

Marple Hall, Cheshire, some claim is where you may see the ghost of Charles II, sometimes in the company of a pretty young woman of origins unknown.

Boscastle in Cornwall is a very interesting place which is allegedly haunted by the ghost of an old witch, so it is not at all surprising that they have a very interesting witchcraft museum. It really is a must for any visitor to Boscastle.

The Witches House at Boscastle, Cornwall, a most magical village if ever there was one

Penryn is also an interesting place and here, I am told, on Christmas Eve and other times a coach and headless black horses are often seen driven by a figure that is little more than a black shadow.

Penzance has a story of an old haunting of a coach and horses and of pirates that slip ashore and yet apparently disappear the instant you see them. Watch for them especially on foggy and misty nights.

A likeness of the phantom hearse at Penzance

Many of you will have visited St Ives for your holiday but did you know that on particularly stormy and windy nights the ghost of a white lady that swings a lantern to warn ships at sea is often seen or that an old ship seen just off the shore that seems to belong to another time is basically just that, a ghost ship.

At Exeter the cathedral cloister is said to have a ghostly occurrence whereby a nun has been seen passing from the south wall of the naive and then to walk straight through other walls in the building. The Deanery apparently also has ghosts - lots of them I am told!
In Plymouth many people say the ghost of Sir Francis Drake still walks. There are many legends that say he was actually a wizard and the area of Plymouth known as Devil's Point is supposed to be a favourite haunt of one of England's great heroes.

Wistman's Wood at Dartmoor has always had legends of strange goings-on. A ghostly rider, a phantom pack of hounds and horses and many other apparitions have been seen in this area and some locals say it is not a place to investigate at night or on your own!

Porlock Hill in Somerset is a scary place to drive your own vehicle up or down - it is so very steep, but several locals have told me a tale of the ghosts of white horses that have been known to charge across the road perhaps making matters more hazardous.

Salisbury Cathedral in Wiltshire is alleged to be haunted and has strange goings-on. Misty figures have been seen walking around the building and there is a legend that tells white birds will always fly three times around the cathedral's spire foretelling the death of important clergy associated with the building.

Stonehenge where many have seen mysterious figures of Druids, especially at dusk and first light.

Scotland

Culzean Castle has the ghostly walk and sound of a Kennedy piper. This is a haunt that has apparently gone on for a very long time indeed. One of my associates Mike McGhee not only claims to have seen him but also says he plays extremely well!

Lochness in Invernesshire is famous for its monster of the deep but it is also haunted they tell me by three ghosts, two young men and a maid who were locked in a love triangle that saw a boy and girl murdered by another. The loch also has strange lights in the hours of darkness that have been described as a misty blue.

Looking out on the haunted, mystical and mysterious lochs of Scotland

Aberdeenshire, Leith Hall, Kennethmont, is said to be the ghostly site of Victorian people not of this world, also a tall, lithesome figure who walks with a limp, sweet-smelling fragrances and the unnerving strains of music.

Iona, this lovely island is the special visit of Christian tourists in their thousands who come to Scotland, but at the northern part of the island, I am told, there have been reports of the ghosts of ancient Druids and even stranger, one correspondent tells me a story of visions of Viking longships just off-shore and of Nordic warriors seen coming ashore and onto the beaches.

Ship to Iona, the Caledonian MacBrayne

Ireland

Moneymore, County Londonderry, Springhill Manor House is said to be haunted by a lady in black clothes, the sound of marching soldiers and the distinct sound of footsteps on the stairs.

Antrim Castle is allegedly haunted by the spectre of a huge wolf-hound, very much like the stone one that is situated just inside the gateway entrance.

Cork, Charles Fort is haunted by a lady in white believed to be a young bride who died in the most tragic of circumstances.

Kilkenny Castle has the legend of being haunted by the spectre of the wife of Strongbow, both over the years have apparently been regularly witnessed.

Wales

Abergele, near Rhyl, Gyrich Castle. The tracks that lead up to this site have given many a visitor a fright. An unseen battle, the clattering of horses hooves and the visions of misty figures. Strange really because the castle is not really old and was built in quite recent times by a gentleman who really did wish to turn his home into a castle.

Gyrich Castle, Abergele, North Wales, where the author himself, on the pathway that leads to it, experienced the paranormal at a very early age

Welshpool, Powys Castle has allegedly at one time claimed to be haunted by a ghostly gentleman in period suit and hat. Others have spoken of the White Lady putting in an appearance on a regular basis..

Mold, Clwyd. At a place called the Hill of Goblins the locals will tell you of the ghost of a ancient warrior dressed in golden armour.

Anglesey is said to be haunted by the figures of ancient Druids and several wild screaming women who wail and throw their hands in the air and have been frequently reported seen in and around the area called Llanddaniel Fab.

Clwyd, Chirk Castle, is said to have a ghost known locally as "the mounted white lady of Chirk", who canters around the surrounding areas on certain nights of the year.

Stonehenge at dusk, a time when some claim the figures of ancient Druids are to be seen amongst the stones

Chapter Five

The Most Haunted House in England's History

Much of this book is to do with the hauntings and ghosts of the English Midlands but one place simply stands out for further investigation and reading if you are interested in the subject, and that is Borley Rectory, which really did deserve the title of the most haunted house in the whole of England. If you are really serious about this subject perhaps at some time in your life you should visit the site and see what you sense for yourself.

The parish church of Borley stands on a hill looking out towards the valley of the River Stour which is the boundary between Essex and Suffolk. Borley Village itself is a fairly small, and on the face of matters, insignificant, but in 1940 a book was published called The Most Haunted House in England. In 1946 an additional book, The End of Borley Rectory was to make this little village famous, or infamous if you prefer, all over the world. Both books were written by the great investigator of the paranormal and ghosts of that time, Harry Price, who, in these books stated that Borley Rectory, an eerie Victorian residence that was burned to the ground in 1939 was the focal point of amazing paranormal occurrences such as a ghostly coach, a ghostly nun, a monk or friar minus his head, the ghost of a former vicar, strange sounding bells, unearthly lights that glow in the dark and water taps that ran thick, black ink.

Borley church a 12th century building was surrounded by very old gravestones was situated on the opposite side of the Sudbury Road to the rectory which burned down in 1939 and was only seventy-five years old at the time, but we are told it always gave off a strange, unexplainable, eerie atmosphere of being very much older. It was actually built in 1863 by the Reverend Henry Bull, a wealthy gent and rector of Borley church, who lived there with his wife and fourteen offspring. Some people claim that the Bull family believed in the legend that a thirteenth century monastery had previously stood on the site of an extension to the rectory built over farm outbuildings and could have been the original home perhaps of the headless monk who had been beheaded for allegedly having a relationship with a nun who is also seen as a ghost. Could this be the reason why the ghost of a nun and other spectres were seen in this area? The Bull family stayed at Borley Rectory for many years until in October, 1928, a new rector, The Reverend G Eric Smith, arrived at Borley. We are told it was a pretty desolate place at that time and it seems the Reverend Smith and his wife were not at all happy. Not only were they quickly told of the legends and ghosts that surround Borley, which in fairness they dismissed, they were continually pestered by the national press for stories. They also admitted that during a seance conducted by Harry Price, the ghost hunter, that communication had been made with the late Harry Bull. Their admission led to Borley being invaded by sightseers once more. It is said that the Reverend Smith and his wife were so upset by this intrusion that employment in another parish was quickly and duly sought and the Smiths moved on in April 1930.

In October 1930, Lionel Foyster, a cousin of Reverend Harry Bull (Henry's son and preceding rector of Borley) became the new rector. Lionel Foyster was to stay at Borley for five years and it is claimed during that time thousands of strange occurrences took place such as strange groaning voices, moving objects, footsteps clearly heard, ghostly apparitions appearing, and messages written on walls in pencil, chalk and other materials. Mrs Marion Foyster, Reverend Lionel's wife, always claimed she felt uneasy and hated Borley.

In October 1935 the Foysters finally left Borley and the Reverend A C Hemming, later that year took up the appointment yet for reasons unknown made the decision to live away from the rectory and for the next few years the house fell into very poor condition. In 1937 Harry Price the ghost hunter rented the building and in a major London newspaper invited people interested in the paranormal or with special gifts to join him spending time studying the house. However, within six months this research came to an end and a military man bought the rectory intending to use it for other purposes. However, in February 1939 this was to prove to be of no avail as fire swept through the rectory reducing the building to little more than ruins.

In 1945, Harry Price wrote another book called The End of Borley Rectory which told further stories of the strange, unexplained happenings that he and others had experienced and was indeed a very popular well read book. Harry Price passed away in 1948 but by now the story of Borley Rectory was famous all over the world but also a site of conjecture and controversy. There are those who have accused Harry Price of embellishing or altering facts or not reporting evidence or investigating things as thoroughly as he might have done, perhaps even hinting that some of the many ghosts of Borley were invented to develop and publicise his own career as the great ghost hunter. Equally, there are those who completely and totally believe that Borley Rectory, the area and other buildings in proximity were undoubtedly the most haunted sites in the world, pointing to the overwhelming evidence and statements from many well respected and investigated statements.

Strangely, in his investigations, Harry Price seemed to pay very little attention to the hauntings across the road at Borley Church, mysterious happenings that go on to this day. In the little churchyard that surrounds the church are the graves of the Bull family, clergy and inhabitants of the most famous building opposite. A lot of psychic investigators in the last few years have looked at the church and its area and have no doubt this is also haunted. It would appear the nun investigated by Price is certainly in and around that vicinity still. Photographs have been taken in the churchyard that apparently show shadows and material that could be described as ectoplasmic. Tape recordings have also been made that have recorded footsteps, large bangs and groaning, grunting voices. even reports of unexplained scribbling appearing in different parts of the village once more similar to that which had once been seen at the rectory itself. If you should be in the vicinity of Borley village the nun is described as being thin, pale with a dark hood and veil.

It is difficult to decide really if Borley is actually haunted or not. I suppose it is very much down to the individual. As a medium and psychic I would have to say that in my opinion it is, and it is one of those sites in the world that has a special atmosphere that sensitives certainly feel. It would appear that the nun has never left, the entity that scribbled and wrote still chooses to do so and there are now stories of phantom horses, strange music and chanting, even ghostly cats and dogs that are seen and heard in and around the vicinity. Of course the site of the rectory itself now lies desolate and bare and is generally avoided by the locals who say strange occurrences still go on.

In summary, I would have to say that Borley will continue to be the focus of attention of those interested in the paranormal for the foreseeable future and continues to be the most famous of haunted places in the world.

Borley Rectory, probably the most investigated haunted building in the world

Chapter Six

Some Royal and Regal Ghosts

Most of the ghosts I tell you about in this book are from the English Midlands but there are times when you want to look at things in another way and one of the interesting ways of looking at ghosts is to think about royal and regal hauntings and ghosts. Throughout history people have claimed to have seen the ghosts of kings and queens of England and it is not unusual really for many of them died in battle violently and of course some were executed so it is not at all strange that the royal family should have quite a history of being haunted and having ghosts. Apparently, the Queen Mother, the Queen and Prince Charles in particular, are all interested in this subject and allegedly Windsor Castle is certainly haunted. Here are just a few royal and regal ghosts that should be of interest to you.

Queen Elizabeth I is said to have been there since 1603 when she died. Some say she still haunts the castle in sorrow and looking for forgiveness for ordering the execution of Mary Queen of Scots. Another famous ghostly visitor is said to be Henry VIII whom people have said they have seen in the area of the cloisters. Henry has also been heard to groan and moan as if in pain and is seen to be dragging one leg behind him. This is not surprising as it is said in life, especially his later life, he often suffered problems with the one leg following a riding accident, and for sure he was cruel to several of his wives. Perhaps he now haunts Windsor in sorrow. One of Henry's wives, Ann Boleyn, has been seen numerous times at the Tower of London, headless and, indeed, on occasions the poor lady has been seen carrying her own severed head in her hands.

The ghost of Charles I is also seen in and around the vicinity of Windsor Castle. The great Tudor palace of Hampton Court is also haunted and is said to be a favourite haunt of Jane Seymour, particularly in the court area. Catherine Howard also walks, or should I say, runs through Hampton Court. Today, rumours abound that even Buckingham Palace may be haunted and that the Queen may have seen the spirit of her father, George VI, on numerous occasions. At Hampton Court in recent years there have been reports of the ghost of Cardinal Wolsey appearing, proudly wearing his red cardinal's gown, perhaps drawn to a time before his position was cruelly taken away from him by King Henry VIII. Lady Jane Grey who was queen for less than a fortnight, has been seen on numerous occasions in the Tower of London, the place of her execution, perhaps re-enacting those awful hours before passing to the higher life.

A royal home that really does have a most strange atmosphere is Glamis Castle in Scotland well known for its association with Shakespeare's play, Macbeth, whilst in truth King Duncan is unlikely to have ever stayed at the castle or to have lost his life there. It is however the family seat of the Bowes-Lyons family ancestors of the present Queen Mother. Legend says a secret chamber hidden somewhere within the castle was the home of a horrible monster, half man, half beast, reputed some say, to have been of aristocratic breeding. There is also a ghost known as the Grey Lady who it is claimed has actually been seen by present members of the royal family kneeling at prayer in the castle's private chapel. Legend has it this lady was a witch and burned at the stake at Edinburgh Castle in 1540. Some say she was the wife of the 6th Lord Glamis.

Really this is just a few of the more royal or regal ghosts I thought I would draw your attention to and there are literally hundreds more that you might like to read about. Look at the history of any castle or great house that aristocratic people have lived in and almost for sure there will be tales, legends and stories of hauntings and ghosts.

Did the Earl of Enville and his lady look something like this?

Chapter Seven

Conclusions

Well, dear reader, you have come to the last section of this book. I do hope you have enjoyed reading about all the ghost stories I have told you, perhaps those of the Midlands in particular. I always remember some twenty or perhaps thirty years ago reading the books of experts in the field myself, and being told the Midlands did not have a great deal of ghosts to tell about, I think we have thoroughly disproved that claim with this book alone, where I have told you about at least one hundred and fifty ghosts in the central areas of England.

**The author on the hunt underneath the arches.
Actually, White Ladies Priory near Boscobel House**

I also thought it was important to include some hauntings for you, although admittedly in smaller numbers, from further afield, in fact right across England, Scotland, Ireland and Wales, so that when you are out and about on your travels you can look up the sites and see what you can learn or, indeed, see or sense because honestly, you will be able to if you are open-minded and believe it is possible. Some of you who have bought this book no doubt will be ghost hunters yourselves or perhaps, and certainly as important to research, doubters and questioners. Do make use of the toolkit I outlined for you in chapter three. It should be invaluable to believers and disprovers equally. I have always openly stated to those who know me well that despite being a professional psychic and medium, I still investigate every snippet of information I am given with an open mind always looking and reasoning with myself that at times things are not what they seem to our normal senses and vision. In years gone by people would tell my mother, a famed Midlands medium, of their stories and I always took it upon myself to disprove any evidence before accepting it to be factual, but there again, then as today, I would come across cases that could not be put down to any rational or scientific answer, basically you just had to accept that what some people call ghosts, hauntings and paranormal experiences, were exactly that and that indeed some people's ghosts were what you could only call ghosts! Nothing else at all would fit the bill, they are ghosts!

Of course, I am quite aware that many of you will read this book just out of interest and for pleasure and let me thank you very much for buying it. Perhaps it will be a pleasant way for you to pass time late at night when the radio and television set have fallen silent or perhaps on a long, lonely train ride that sees you travelling many miles without any company at all. If in situations like this and whilst reading my book you suddenly find a bang or a fleeting vision of light that makes you suddenly sit bolt upright, prick up your ears or keep looking behind you, of course a sensible person like yourself will say, "I am just letting my imagination get to me," and of course you are probably quite right. However, next time a figure of perhaps what seems to be an everyday normal person walks past you but just doesn't seem quite right, even when it is broad daylight and simply just vanishes in the twinkling of an eye, I think you ought to give consideration to the fact that you might have just seen a ghost. Even then, remind yourself that out of every hundred cases ninety-nine will have a perfectly rational explanation.

This book, the same as any other book on the subject that you may read, should only be seen as a guide. Always let yourself be the witness that you most believe in. Always keep in mind that old saying we all know well, "I will believe it when I see with my own eyes," for in my experience that is the only way that anyone will ever really believe in ghosts. Therefore, I wish you good luck and, of course, good ghost hunting.

The End

Excellent Books to Read/
Bibliography/Acknowledgments

Ghosts of the Midlands and How to Detect Them (1990). Philip Solomon.
Ghosts, Legends and Psychic Snippets (1991). Philip Solomon.
Black Country Ways in Bygone Days (1992). Philip Solomon.
The Good Ghost Guide (1992). Philip Solomon.
The Great Midland Ghost Guide (1993). Philip Solomon.
Dreamers Psychic Dictionary (1994). Philip Solomon.
Railway Ghosts (1985). W B Herbert.
Night Side of Nature, or Ghosts and Ghost-Seers (1986). Catherine Crowe.
Ghosts of Yorkshire (1987). William Reginald Mitchell.
Our Neighbourly Ghosts. Doreen Evelyn.
Ghosts of Cumbria's Castles and Halls (1984). Margaret Campbell.
Ghosts of London. West End, South and West (1982). J A Brooks.
Ghosts Over Britain (1979). Peter Moss.
Stately Ghosts of England (1977). Diana Norman.
The University of Spiritualism. Harry Boddington.
Science and Parascience (1984). Brian Inglis.
Photographing The Invisible (1911).* James Coates.
Ghosts of an Ancient City (1974). John Vincent Mitchell.
Realm of Ghosts (1971). Eric Maple.
Mysteries (1978). Collin Wilson.
One Hundred Cases for Survival After Death (1943).* A T Baird.
Seers, Psychics and ESP (1970). Milbourne Christopher.
The Poltergeist (1972). William G Roll.
A Host of Hauntings (1973). Peter Underwood.
On the Edge of the Etheric. Arthur Findlay.
Understanding Ghosts (1980). Victoria Branden.
Great British Ghosts (1980). Aidan Chambers.
Haunted Ireland: Her Romantic and Mysterious Ghosts (1977). John Dunne.
Visions. Apparitions. Alien Visitors. Hilary Evans.
Some Ghosts of Staffordshire. (1981) Rosalind Prince.
Real Ghosts, Restless Spirits and Haunted Minds (1968). Brad Steiger.
Ghosts of The South East (1976). Andrew Green.
Ghosts in Solid Form (1914).* Gambier Bolton.
Hauntings: New Light on 10 Famous Cases (1977). Peter Underwood.
Ghosts (1984). Orbis Publishing.

Lancashire's Ghosts and Legends (1982).* Terence Whitaker.
The Way of Life. Arthur Findlay.
Through the Time Barrier. Danah Zohar.
Haunted London (1973). Peter Underwood.
Ghosts of Glasgow (1983). William W Barr.
Ghosts and Legends of the Lake District (1988). J A Brooks.
The Second Book of Irish Ghost Stories (1971). Patrick Burn.
The Ghost Hunters Strangest Cases (1975). Hans Holzer.
Great Hauntings (1988). Peter Brookesmith.
A Ghost Hunters Handbook (1980). Peter Underwood.
Ghosts and Legends (1994). Peter Walters.
Appearances of the Dead : Cultural History of Ghosts (1982). Ronald E Finucane.
True Irish Ghost Stories (1969). Seymour and Nelligan.
Supernature (1973). Lyall Watson.
Psychic Photography (1970). Hans Holzer.
Poltergeists and Hauntings (1965). David Cohen.
Mysterious Worlds (1970). Dennis Bardens.
The Ghost Hunter's Road Book (1968). John Harries.
The Undiscovered Country. Howard Murphet.
The History of Spiritualism. Sir Arthur Conan Doyle.
Life After Life. Raymond A Moody.
Dictionary of Ghosts (1982). Peter Haining.
Lancashire Ghosts (1979). Kathleen Eyre.
Secret Britain (1968). G Bernard Wood.
Beyond Explanation? (1985). Jenny Randles.
Is Anybody There? (1980). Stewart Lamont.
Ghosts of Wales (1978). Peter Underwood.
Ghosts of Hampshire and the Isle of Wight (1983). Peter Underwood.
Apparitions and Ghosts (1971).* Andrew MacKenzie.
Ghosts Over Britain (1979).* Peter Moss.
Clairvoyant Reality. Lawrence LeShan.
The Ghosts of Trianon. Michael H Coleman.
The Queen Mother's Family Story (1967). J W Day.
The Table Rappers (1972). Ronald Pearsall.
In Search of the Supernatural (1975). Peter Travis.
Hauntings and Apparitions. Andrew MacKenzie.
Ghosts of the North Country (1974).* Henry Tegner.
Ghosts of the South East (1981).* Andrew Green.

Ghosts of Old England (1987). Terence W Whitaker.
Psychic Phenomena in Ireland (1972). Sheila St. Clair.
Afterlife (1985). Colin Wilson.
The Ghosts Who's Who (1977). Jack Hallam.
Queen Victoria's Other World. Peter Underwood.
Photographing the Spirit World. Cyril Permutt.
Ghosts of London. East End, City and North (1982). J A Brooks.
Local Ghosts (1976). Margaret Royal and Ian Girvan.
Unfamiliar Spirits: Ghosts of the British Isles (1989). Keith B. Poole.
Ghosts: The Illustrated History (1975).* Peter Haining.
Ghosts of the Tower of London (1989). G. S. Abbot.
Ghosts, Spirits and Spectres of Scotland (1973). Francis Thompson.
Ghosts of London (1975). Jack Hallam.
Death-bed Visions. Sir William Barratt.
The Unexplained (1966). A MacKenzie.
Beyond the Senses (1971) Paul Tabori.
Ghosts of Dorset, Devon and Somerset (1974). Rodney Legg.
Parapsychology (The controversial science) (1991). Richard Broughton.
Ghosts I Have Seen and Other Psychic Experiences (1986). Violet Tweedale.
Historic Houses and Castles Guide (1994). RAC.
Haunted House Handbook (1978) D Scott Rogo.
Victorian Ghosts (1973). Hans Holzer.
World's Greatest Ghosts (1982). Nigel Blundell and Roger Boar.
Some Ghostly Tales of Shropshire (1988). Christine McCarthy.
When Dead Kings Speak. Tony Ortzen.
The Story of the Poltergeist Down the Centuries (1953).* Hereward Carrington and Nandor Fodor.
The Guinness Encyclopaedia of Ghosts and Spirits (1994). Rosemary Guiley.
Haunted Warwickshire (1981). May Elizabeth Atkins.
Ghosts and Poltergeists (1976). Frank Smith.
Yorkshire Ghosts and Legends (1983).* Terence W Whitaker.
Dictionary of the Supernatural (1978). Peter Underwood.
Ghosts and Legends of the Wiltshire Countryside (1973).* Kathleen Wiltshire and Patricia Carrott.
Historic British Ghosts (1974). Philip W Sargeant.
Lakeland Ghosts (1984).* Gerald Findler.
Ghosts of the Lake Counties (1989).* Gerald Findler.
Ghosts of Wessex (1977).* Keith B Poole.
Gazetteer of British Ghosts (1971).* Peter Underwood.

Gazetteer of Scottish and Irish Ghosts (1973).* Peter Underwood and Paul Tabori.
The A to Z of British Ghosts (1992). Peter Underwood.
Ghosts of Derbyshire (1973).* Clarence Daniel.
Theatre Ghosts (1988). Roy Harley Lewis.
Ghosts of East Anglia (1984). H Mills West.
North Country Ghosts and Legends (1988). Terence W Whitaker.
Ghosts of Staffordshire.* Rosalind Prince.
Ghosts of Dorset (1988). Peter Underwood.
True Experiences With Ghosts (1979).* Martin Ebon.
Ghosts (1970).* Eric Russell.
Ghosts of Yorkshire (1982).* William Reginald Mitchell.
Yorkshire Ghosts (1977).* William Reginald Mitchell.
Ghosts of the Chiltern and Thames Valley (1983). Hilary Stainer Rice.
Ghosts and Hauntings in Beverley and East Riding (1987). Peter H Robinson and Paul A Hesp.
Liverpool Ghosts and Ghouls (1986). Richard Whittington-Egan.
Ghosts of the Forest of Dean (1983). Sue Law.
Real Ghosts (1970).* Brad Steiger.
Haunted Britain (1973). Anthony D Hippsley Coxe.
Ghosts of the North (1976).* Jack Hallam.
Ghosts in the South West (1973).* James Turner.
Do you Believe in Ghosts? (1987). Joycelyn Bell.
The Geller Effect (1986). Uri Geller and Guy Lyon Playfair.
This House is Haunted (1980). Guy Lyon Playfair.
Are You Psychic? (1997). Hans Holzer.

* Out of Print.

Special thanks to Duckworth Publishers for permission to reproduce photograph of Borley Rectory. Original rights untraceable.

First class magazines and papers:
    (In the USA) - Fate Magazine
    (In Great Britain) - Prediction Magazine, Psychic News, The Greater World